SUBWAY LINE, No. 11

D0910416

Upper West Side Philosophers, Inc. provides a
publication venue for original philosophical thinking
steeped in lived life, in line with our motto:
philosophical living & lived philosophy.

passing time

Andrea Köhler With a foreword by **Mark Lilla**

an essay
on waiting

Translated from the German by
Michael Eskin

Upper West Side Philosophers, Inc. New York

Published by Upper West Side Philosophers, Inc.
P. O. Box 250645, New York, NY 10025, USA
www.westside-philosophers.com

English Translation and Foreword Copyright © 2011, 2017
by Upper West Side Philosophers, Inc.

Passing Time: An Essay on Waiting was originally published in
German as *Lange Weile: Über das Warten* Copyright © Insel
Verlag Frankfurt und Leipzig 2007

Yoga for the Mind©

The colophon is a registered trademark of
Upper West Side Philosophers, Inc.

Library of Congress Cataloging-in-Publication Data

Names: Köhler, Andrea, author. | Eskin, Michael, translator.
  | Lilla, Mark, writer of supplementary content.
Title: Passing time : an essay on waiting / Andrea Köhler;
  with a foreword by Mark Lilla ; translated from the German
  by Michael Eskin.
Other titles: Lange Weile. English
Description: New York : Upper West Side Philosophers,
  Inc., 2017. | Series: Subway line ; No. 11 | Includes biblio-
  graphical references.
Identifiers: LCCN 2016034606 | ISBN 9781935830481
  (pbk. : alk. paper)
Subjects: LCSH: Waiting (Philosophy) | Time.
Classification: LCC B105.W24 K6413 2017 |
  DDC 115--dc23
LC record available at https://lccn.loc.gov/2016034606

For the one,

and

for her, who first kept me waiting

CONTENTS

FOREWORD

Socrates is waiting. Ordinarily a man convicted of a capital offense—in this case, impiety and corrupting the young—would be executed immediately. But the Athenians think it inauspicious to put anyone to death during the annual mission to Delos, and the ship hasn't returned yet. So Socrates waits, and his friends wait with him.

To pass the time they talk. This conversation seems different from earlier ones, though, more earnest and emotional. One man cries. They all know how the day will end, and why, so they have come to mourn. But Socrates won't allow it. He feigns surprise at their sadness and demands an account, though he knows perfectly well what's going on. They are anxious about their own deaths, not his.

But why? They talk and talk. The hours pass and still his friends can't give him a rational explanation for their fear. Each time they offer one, Socrates shoots it down. They begin to wonder whether anyone really knows for certain what happens to our souls after we die—or, for that matter, whether they existed before we were born. Socrates is pleased; uncertainty is progress. Now he can take the conversation in hand and drive it to the conclusion they've reached many times before, that it's not important when or how death comes, but how we live in light of it. That's what philosophy is about. It is "practice for dying and being dead." If a man stays true to her, he tells them, always questioning himself and others, his soul will be transported to a blessed land, free from body and time. Whether Socrates convinces his friends of this is uncertain. But he reveals something else just by sitting there with them. They learn through experience that waiting inspires philosophy, and that philosophy in turn gives meaning to the wait. The *Phaedo* enacts the very lesson it imparts. It is Plato's most beautiful dialogue.

Man is the waiting animal. That is the golden sentence in Andrea Köhler's beautiful essay on the experience of waiting, which made a deep impression on me when it originally appeared in German. She is too modest to call it a philosophical work, but I am not. English and American philosophers write about subjective human experiences like love and anger more than they used to, but their interests are mainly ethical and their imaginative range narrow. They are so eager to draw lessons that they tend to ignore the texture of the experiences, leaving that to novelists and poets and filmmakers, whom they dutifully footnote. One pleasure in reading certain continental philosophers—think of Nietzsche, Bergson, Husserl, Heidegger, Benjamin, Sartre—is how they tarry with subjectivity and its paradoxes. Their first question about an experience is, *what is it like?*, not *what does it imply?* That is how Andrea Köhler begins her inquiry, by asking a seemingly simple question: what exactly is it to wait?

Not long into this small book you realize how little you've thought about it. Yet in a sense all we do is wait. We wait for good things to begin and to end, we wait for bad things to begin and to end. The thoughts and feelings we have are not simple, nor are they the same in these four cases. Sometimes we wait in fear, sometimes we're bored or anxious; sometimes our minds turn toward the past, more often we struggle to forget. We day-dream, we have insights, we make resolutions—school's out. And then there are waits we don't want to end, that are pleasures in themselves. Think of a child's joy in the month before Christmas, and the melancholy that sets in once it's past. The holiday never measures up, not because children's expectations are too high but because the wait is so fun.

It's like that for adults, too, after making love, when the dance of seduction is over and the musicians are packing up their instruments. The older you get, the more volup-tuous that state of *attente* can be. Some-times—try explaining this to a sixteen-year-old—consummation seems beside the point. We all have our idiosyncrasies when it comes to waiting. I'm very bad at it, except when I'm about to make a long journey. I arrange to get my packing done a day early so I can spend the hours before departure in that peaceful zone of pure anticipation. Because I've removed the armor of daily life but haven't yet put on my psychic traveling suit, I float in a kind of reverie. It's happened that after getting to the airport and hearing my gate called, I've been tempted to turn back and just head home. I've already gotten what I came for.

The art of waiting needs to be learned. Socrates believed you cannot live a good life without it. This same thought appears, in somewhat different forms, in ancient Stoicism, Jewish messianism, Christian mysticism, Montaigne, Pascal, and Kierkegaard. Köhler, with a gentle nod to Heidegger, sees waiting as a kind of letting go, a precious *Gelassenheit* that allows us to feel time, not just think it. In waiting, and perhaps only in waiting, we experience ourselves as temporal creatures, who both live in the moment and project ourselves into the future. We then experience our very selves. Just as no one can take a bath for you, no one can wait for you. The child who cries when his mother leaves the room gets his first lesson in life: we wait alone. Köhler likens our condition to that of Scheherazade, whose life hangs in the balance for 1001 nights as she tells King Shahryar tales; or Penelope planted before her loom, weaving and unweaving without end. We become ourselves by filling the time.

But we can also get beyond ourselves, if we know how. Andrea Köhler wants to persuade us that learning to wait can open the soul to surprise, to wonder, to what Christian theologians call the *kairos*, the moment in time that breaks through time, reorienting it. In the blink of an eye we experience our time as gift, as miracle. Just let go, she says, and wander:

> That all roads are, in some way, also detours
> we feel in places like Venice or Lisbon,

where most lanes and alleys end at city walls, bridges, or canals. How could we bear life without travel, which reminds us that sometimes we must get lost to get where, without knowing it, we want to be: this piazza, that façade, or that enchanted panorama we would not have found without making a wrong turn. But roaming is also an end in itself. It follows the distant call of mysterious voices, children playing, the peal of bells of borrowed time. Only one ready to lose himself in the labyrinth enters into the dream that a place dreams of itself …

Wise advice for those who would practice living and being alive.

Mark Lilla

PREFACE

On Waiting

Waiting is an imposition. Yet only waiting in its manifold guises—in traffic or love, at the gate or the doctor's—affords us an embodied sense of time and its promises. *We wait*: for spring and the jackpot, for the food, for an offer, for *the one* and Godot— for test results, happiness, birthdays, and laughs—for a call, for what's next, for the knock on the door—for the pain to subside and the storm to blow over ... Idleness, by- ways, detours, and boredom—waiting is the page in the book of planned hours that needs to be filled. With luck, its reward will be freedom.

I love the transitions, the liminal states, the hours undefined—for a while, anyway— the twilight that heralds the night, which, in turn, promises more than just morning's re- turn. Those who can wait know well what it means to live in the conditional tense. However, if fooled by false hopes we don't make our choices, insisting on 'keeping our options open', we'll easily miss opportunity's call and let life pass us by. Such sins of omission are the stuff of literature, which is ruled by an economy of attention whose costs and benefits cannot be gauged by the standards of our fast-paced, over-committed everyday lives, and which enjoins us—as already Seneca noted—to spend our time in meaningful and hopefully also fulfilling ways.

There is no growth, no development without waiting—think of pregnancy, puberty, or the strains of creative labor. Maybe that's what Franz Kafka meant when he referred to his own life as a "hesitation before birth." Waiting means imagining what might or might not happen. Moreover, insofar as it implies keeping desire in check it lies, as Sigmund Freud has suggested, at the root of all symbolic communion and can thus be considered humanity's first major cultural achievement.

If we think of life as an irregular concatenation of instants, including those moments when the steady flow of expectation is suddenly interrupted and we feel stuck, then these temporary breaks will appear above all as congestions or interferences in the world of chronic simultaneity we have created at the expense of the open-ended, undulating rhythms of time unfolding. Still, within the high-speed worlds of affluent societies, oases of slowness have emerged—from memorial sites to spas—designed to restore a different measure of time to the 'hurtling standstill' of our age. Most of these 'islands of rest', however, have something artificial about them, for there is no way back to paradise, which, all promises of salvation notwithstanding, was never to be had in this life anyway. Even a trip around the world will neither relieve us of time's pressures nor lead us to heaven's gate, as Heinrich von Kleist imagined. At best, we may wind up on an island that vaguely resembles our idea of earthly bliss. Life's most mysterious 'island of rest', its most enigmatic break, is undoubtedly sleep —our nightly exercise in waiting, from which we will one day no longer awaken.

We can never shake the constitutive duality of our existence, indelibly marked as it is by the unremitting interplay between sleeping and waking, absence and presence, the not-yet and the no-longer. Music may have given the most palpable expression to this duality, even though its rhythms, rests, and repetitions follow patterns that are more predictable than life's vagaries.

I have tried to echo the rhythms of expectation and waiting by punctuating my reflections with fictional interludes spoken by an 'I' not unlike the author's, who, I must confess, considers herself a member of that 'laggard species' that is all too often guilty of tardiness. Which is to say: I wrote this book without the slightest sense of nostalgia or cultural lament, and with the hope of bringing out the joyful aspects of waiting, slowness, and rest.

Of the promise of salvation, the coming of the messiah, and the utopian dream of paradise on earth I will treat only marginally—these forms of expectation involve general questions of faith any speculation on which will most likely be a foregone conclusion to the true believer. What I am interested in is the kind of waiting that falls squarely within the realm of individual experience, which, in today's world, faces the paradox of an overabundance of too little time.

Homo sapiens is the *waiting animal* capable of anticipating death. Even as unpredictability is gradually eliminated from our lives (or so it seems) due to ever-shortening wait times and the vanishing of in-between spaces, our parting rituals, too—from the simple 'so long' to the performance of last rites—adapt to the pressures of a restless world. There was a time when each parting contained a 'small death', in the sense of a strong chance of never seeing each other again or losing touch for good. But since technology has made it possible to stay connected at all times, we can barely imagine what it might mean no longer to be around one day. Waiting is a state in which time holds its breath in order to remind us of our mortality. Its motto is not *carpe diem* but *memento mori*.

Prelude

I Wait

For a long time I just kept lying and waiting. For what? For the day outside to assume a different hue and the noises to inspire me to try my hand at verticality? For the force of habit to break my morning resistance to stepping through day's door and being a person again, walking on two legs, with a birth certificate, profession, and address? Why not simply wait for this listless phase to pass? And already I'm wondering: am I waiting for some-thing to happen, or perhaps for something to cease? Maybe it's the same thing—something stops be-cause it is displaced by something else waiting to happen—somewhere, beyond the seven hills of time. The more anxiously I expect it, the more I am haunted by it. The one waiting is in a peculiar sit-uation: fastened to the rack of time, he is himself the red carpet in the halls of expectation longing for the first footfall. Waiting means being no stranger to paradox.

I. ANXIETY

Where Are You?

> The lover's fatal identity is to be the one waiting.
>
> (Roland Barthes)

At the beginning of *Speak, Memory*, Vladimir Nabokov depicts a "chronophobiac who experienced something like panic" when watching for the first time "homemade movies that had been taken a few weeks before" he was born: "He saw a world that was practically unchanged—the same house, the same people—and then realized that he did not exist there at all and that nobody mourned his absence." Among other things, he was disturbed by the "unfamiliar gesture" of his mother "waving from an upstairs window," which felt to him like "some mysterious farewell." What particularly frightened him, however, was "the sight of a brand-new baby carriage standing there on the porch, with the smug, encroaching air of a coffin [and] empty, as if, in the reverse course of events, his very bones had disintegrated."

"The cradle rocks above an abyss," Nabokov writes, and even though our existence may be "but a brief crack of light between two eternities of darkness," the end before us appears more terrifying to us than our once not-yet-having-been. It's as though something were awaiting us in the future—a 'nothingness' (whatever it may be) that we have actually long since left behind. Isn't our whole life a kind of waiting for something that fell into oblivion with our first cry?

"WAIT, verb: look out (for), watch, direct one's attention, care, tend, serve, bide one's time" reads the definition in the Grimm Brothers' classical dictionary, according to which the expression *to wait for someone*, in the present-day sense, first appeared in the sixteenth century. A quick glance at the dictionary, furthermore, reveals that the changes in the word's meaning over time themselves already bespeak a long history of waiting. *Waiting* in the sense of *serving* once articulated a power structure that, in its most civilized form, still resonates in such expressions as *to wait* or *attend upon*; it survives most conspicuously in the *waiter*'s trade, which is, ironically, the exact opposite of *waiting for* in that it implies *abiding* presence as well as *watching* or *looking out for*. *Waiting* in the common modern sense was apparently first recorded as far back as the thirteenth century. Not until the eighteenth century, however, did it accrue those adverbial facets and specifications that testify to its more painful side. Since the age of Romanticism, one waits *with longing*, *impatience*, or *in agony*.

Perhaps that's why the helplessness that often accompanies waiting is best described in physical terms: *it hurts*, our body cramps up, we feel achy, as if from a cold draught caused by doors left ajar. Waiting has a temperature—we can remain cool, or burn with desire. What it is exactly that hurts—making waiting, literally, *a pain*—is more difficult to grasp, for waiting is both imaginary and concrete: a vision of something potentially real that is being withheld.

If the person we are waiting for happens to be someone we love, expectation can easily turn into longing, and longing escalate into mad desire. So intense can the experience of waiting become when love is involved that it will affect our whole being, for love is haunted by the fear of separation and loss. "The cradle rocks above an abyss," and the one waiting can't help being reminded about it.

According to French philosopher Roland Barthes, the lover is always "the one waiting," the one who can't afford to be late—after all, longing, anxiety's sister, is punctual: "Am I in love? Yes, since I'm the one waiting—the other never waits. How I'd love to play the part of the one not waiting sometimes! Even if I try keeping myself so busy as not to be able to avoid being late, though, I always lose at this game; whatever I do, I arrive on time, if not early, finding myself idly waiting." The lover's punctuality betrays his weakness; and in case the other is indeed late, the roles are clearly assigned, for the time being anyway: the one waiting is by definition the one who loves more. Condemned to stay put in view of the other's absence—"all expectation, available … like an unclaimed package in some God-forsaken corner of a railway station"—he always unconsciously reckons with the possibility of having been abandoned. A lover's waiting is directly related to the *primal scene*, the overwhelming first experience of the mother's absence. Only a brief instant presumably separates the moment when the child believes his mother to be merely absent from the moment when it thinks she is dead. Whenever we have to wait for someone we love, we are subcutaneously thrown back upon this experience. Thus, waiting evokes the curse of a threat going back to childhood.

Our modes of coping with anxiety, too, go back to a past when waiting constituted an existential crisis. In a famous passage, Freud describes what he takes to be his little grandson's attempts to cope with his mother's absence by playing a game. The game consists in "throwing away from himself any small objects he can find" and accompanying this activity with a "loud, drawn-out *o-o-o-o*," which the mother takes to mean *gone*. Based on this, Freud conjectures that his grandson is using his toys to play *gone*, thereby transforming himself from a victim into an agent who actively stages his mother's absence and return. "One day," Freud writes, "I made an observation that confirmed my view. The child had a wooden reel with a string attached to it, but it never occurred to him to pull it behind him across the floor, for instance, and pretend that it was a wagon. What he did instead was to hold the reel by the string and skillfully cast it into his curtained bed, thus making it disappear, all the while uttering his expressive *o-o-o-o*. He would then pull the reel out again and greet its reappearance with a joyful *there*. That was the entire game, disappearance and return."

Such wooden reels, which enable us to play the game of *gone/there* on our own terms, are part and parcel of all scenarios of waiting. The one waiting sets up an imaginary stage, and on it he performs a *soliloquy of expectation* rife with emotions whose depth and nuances depend on our relationship with the one for whom we happen to be waiting.

According to Roland Barthes, there is something like a "dramaturgy of waiting" that tends to follow a classical pattern. Let's take a situation in which a person we love is running late. At first, we'll probably come up with plausible reasons for his tardiness—*the subway has been delayed, or he might have been held up at the office, something unexpected that couldn't wait must have come up*; we might then get annoyed because *he's late again!*, before mentally going over the date, place, and time of our rendezvous—*Monday, 3:30, at our favorite coffee shop … are we sure about this? Yes, it's where we met last time*—besides, leaving our spot to check if he might actually be waiting for us at the café across the street would mean risking missing him should he arrive *here* while we look over *there … Thank god for cell phones!* we might then think, nipping all our doubts in the bud … *But—what if we only get his voicemail?* And so our soliloquy spirals along to the point of hysterics: *and what if something has happened to him?* If we're lucky,

reason takes over, but only at the cost of disappointment, which cannot fail promptly to
set in, tinged with the nagging suspicion that
he might not be showing us sufficient respect. In the end, though, anxiety wins the
day: *and what if he never shows up?* Better to
think of something else until he arrives and
we can greet him with a reproach, or, better
yet, with the grand gesture of absolution.

   This one-man show is but an adult version
of the child's *gone/there* game minus the
wooden reel, stuffed animals, and other *transitional objects* that patiently taught us the art
of waiting (and that some of us never grow
out of). Marking the threshold between inside and outside, absence and presence, these
objects quintessentially embody the hope for
our mother's return. In the "monologue of
absence" playing out in the mind of the one
anxiously waiting the other is *there* insofar as
I'm thinking of him, and he is *gone* insofar as
I'm inevitably thrown back upon myself in
the solitude of my waiting: "This singular dis-
tortion makes for an unbearable present,"
Barthes remarks, "I'm wedged between two

modes of temporality, that of *reference* and that of *address*—in my complaints *he* is gone, but in my address *you* are there—and so I learn what the present, that difficult tense, is: a pure slice of anxiety."

Perhaps, waiting might be best described as a continuous reenactment of the primal scene of abandonment, as the infinite deferral of a separation that has always already taken place. *I, here—you, there*. Fastened to the rack of uncertainty, the one waiting feels the power of time minute by grueling minute. The longer he waits, the smaller he gets, eventually shrinking to the size of a single, red-hot point: *never again!*

The Silence of the Sirens

Please, God, let him telephone me now.
(Dorothy Parker)

Before the invention of the cordless telephone, waiting for a call epitomized love—unrequited love, for the most part. Literature had appropriated this motif since the very beginnings of telecommunication. Waiting, after all, is an integral part of love's imaginary, and longing the essence of imagination. From Jean Cocteau's play *The Human Voice*, to Dieter Wellershoff 's novella *The Siren*, to Nicholson Baker's novel *Vox*, the modern Odysseus has been tied to a telephone pole, exposed to the "sad, powerful song" that already Franz Kafka heard emanating from his receiver a century ago.

Even the advent of cellular phones hasn't liberated us from the captivity of waiting. To be sure, the one waiting for a call is no longer glued to the telephone, conjuring it as if in a magic ritual. But anyone who can barely wait for his cell phone to ring in his pocket is like a circus horse obediently trotting out its laps in the arena, having fallen under the spell of the "silence of the sirens," which Kafka, for one, considered "far more pernicious than their irresistible song."

Anxiously waiting for the other to call— suspended between passivity and action— we put ourselves partially at his mercy. We can try to do something to relieve the tension, to bridge the silence with our own precarious words. When no one talks to us, we begin to 'self-soothe'. Like children, who still believe in the magic power of language, we can tell ourselves not to worry: the more dire the situation, the more ardent our prayers, and the greater the certainty that our wish will be heard. We can still observe this kind of behavior in those embarrassing moments when we tacitly ask for succor from above in the impossible hope that the universe might actually be ruled by magic. Waiting turns into incantation and, eventually, litany: *Dear God, the child in us begs, make this waiting stop—please, make it go away!*

When our patience is tried, we tend to fall back on infantile coping mechanisms. Perhaps that's why we often become so childish when we have to wait. Nobody has captured the tragicomic aspects of this motif as pointedly as Dorothy Parker in her short story *A Telephone Call*—that classic monologue by the telephone, which is but an extended variation on this one supplication: "Please, God, let him telephone me now."

In the drama of waiting, the telephone remains a central prop. By allowing us to hear and feel the other's breathing and voice as if he were next to us, it's the only device capable of conjuring real presence and intimacy across long distances, affording us the illusion that we haven't been left. Just like Freud's wooden reel with a string attached to it, which presumably helped his grandson to cope with his mother's absence, telecommunication, too, is a kind of umbilical cord designed to defy separation and bespeaking the paradoxical experience of presence-in-absence accompanied by impatience. Probably, that's why even as patient a character as the narrator of Marcel Proust's *In Search of Lost Time* cannot but immediately complain whenever the connection doesn't work.

Whoever even bothers to complain about bad service nowadays, though, will most likely be put on hold: "Please, wait for the next available representative" will be his provider's song. All the while, the one waiting remains superstitious, haunted by the eerie suspicion that the other *can't get through be-*

cause I'm on hold, or that he'll call as soon as I step out, or, better yet, *have no reception*. French critic Maurice Blanchot once spoke of "the sheer suspense of waiting" coupled with "the blissful disappointment of waiting"—which might suggest that the experience of waiting holds valuable lessons for both our fears and our hopes. Doesn't the one waiting repeat the same tune over and over again: *forbearance is no acquittance?*

Interlude

Future Perfect

It was late afternoon on a gloomy November day, and I decided not to go home that night. I got on the bus and took in the antiquated charm of the French bourgeoisie through the illuminated windows—stucco, chandeliers, mirrors—the ivory nostalgia of a tradition barely kept alive. Rue Coulaincourt—the last stop of a memory. When I entered the Bar au Rêve, I was greeted by the proprietor standing under an old photograph. She still had the same graceful smile as in the picture, which

35

showed her leaning on a man wearing a beret and with a cigarette in his mouth—a happy couple in a distant Paris moment frozen into a memento of love a quarter of a century ago.

Back then, I was lonely, drifting aimlessly from affair to affair. I would often sit on the worn banquette in the farthest corner of the café, watching the entrance, waiting for something to happen that would put an end to my disappointments. I had been sitting like this for an hour when suddenly I saw her reflection in the window. Without looking up, I followed her every move along the arc of my inner tension. She was standing at the bar in the company of a much older man—a glass of red wine in front of her, behind her a history that seemed to synchronize the smiles of this unequal couple. Instantly, I felt terribly jealous, watching her from my hiding place, furtively and as if already found out. For a brief moment, I thought I might have confused her with someone else. For though it was her face, it was somehow distorted—as in a dream—by the memory of a lost intimacy that had already anticipated the erosion of the years ahead when we first touched each other. Suddenly, I was catapulted back in time, seeing her again as on the day we'd met. Today, I sometimes think that it was already over before it had even begun—a foregone conclusion to nothing. We'd only have to stop pretending and admit: never again will I be able to wait for you.

Just You Wait

We usually wait because we are forced to, not because we want to; sometimes, tough —depending on the situation, or because we are compelled by prudence or pride—we *decide* to wait, even though this may go against our individual sense of time. For all waiting is heteronomous, or, at the very least, occasioned by conditions not entirely of our own choosing. Let's assume that we are anxiously waiting for our lover to call after a fight. Since we probably don't want to admit that we have become so dependent, we try to convince ourselves that we can stop waiting any time. We come up with explanations, without believing them; we attempt to suppress our emotions and be reasonable, telling ourselves, *That's it, I've had it!* But this only works if we've already anticipated the possibility that things are over. We imagine the other withdrawing more and more without ever learning exactly why. We submit to the future and resign ourselves to waiting in the face of the irreversible separation we have conjured. It's as if, in this choreography of loss, the other's absence had already taken place within us.

Then, again, we might be racked by impatience, feel trampled on and deserted. How long before impatience turns to anger, and anger to thoughts of revenge? And already the scenario of our own withdrawal has begun unfolding on love's imaginary stage: *just you wait ... soon you'll be the one waiting!* The question is how much of this psychodrama, in which we'll never see each other again, our love can possibly sustain.

2. FEELING

Until Tomorrow

According to essayist Wilhelm Genazino, "children are particularly good at waiting because they aren't yet suspicious of it and don't feel the need to judge it for its presumed lack of cultural value." While it may be true that children don't yet consider waiting a waste of time, this doesn't mean that they don't experience the many situations in which they are made to wait as disempowering at the very least. From adapting to schedules devised by others, to learning to control our bowel movements, to adjusting our circadian rhythms to the rule of night and day —the first power struggles in our lives take place on the battlefield of waiting; they are all about encoding the body, whipping it into conformity with the clock, being drilled into patience.

Learning to wait may well be the "basic condition" for the child's entry into the "world of understanding and reason," insofar as both imply continuity, as Genazino suggests. Interestingly, though, the child also experiences waiting as something discontinuous and limited, having a clear beginning and an end. Because the child's attention is still completely "wrapped up in the moment," to quote Friedrich Nietzsche, waiting for it is but a bounded concatenation of indefinite instants. Which is why children don't yet suspect any 'foul play' while patiently waiting through many a delay in the course of their day—often daydreaming away the hours free of adult demands and creating their own realities. Thus, waiting can be considered our first exercise in utopian thinking, in resisting others managing our lives.

That's not to say, however, that as children we may not also have experienced time as excruciatingly long. How could we ever forget the never-ending adult conversations we had to sit through, or the grueling boredom of all those visits to relatives with nothing to do but stay put and wait for it to be over—childhood tortures that sometimes still haunt us in our dreams. But it was also during those painful stretches of enforced patience, when we couldn't wait to get out and be free again, that we first developed an embodied sense of time, which felt like a persistent, dull pressure in our guts, an aching sensation affecting our whole body. The minutes morphed into gooey strands of gum, the body turned into a rack ... And what about all those times when we wished for nothing more than infinite delay, when our hearts began racing at the very thought that something we had done might soon be discovered, when all we would pray for was the eternity of the *not-yet* in which our 'crime' would magically expire?

Childhood is steeped in rituals of waiting. Think of all the birthdays and Christmases we could barely wait for to arrive, all the excitement about presents we had to wait to open *until tomorrow*—textbook examples of moments of joyful expectation that we tend to idealize, turning them into beacons of nostalgia for a time when expectation and excitement were presumably still one. Yet, in all this, there was also a pedagogical dimension. The interdiction contained in every *not until tomorrow* suggests that childhood's havens of expectation are never completely safe. Even the innocuous and beloved childhood ritual of opening the flaps of the advent calendar in the weeks before Christmas is premised on the coupling of promise and prohibition—the promise of a treat on each day of advent and the injunction not to open the flaps before the respective date each has been assigned. Should the temptation to disregard the prohibition turn out to be more powerful than our patience, then we must learn the hard way that whoever can't wait is his own worst enemy, robbing himself of the sweet rewards of patience.

Waiting to Die

In a memorable passage, Austrian author Peter Handke depicts the child's experience of waiting as a sudden attack of an all-encompassing tiredness. He remembers how once, as a child, during Christmas mass, he was overcome by a tiredness that "struck with the force of a malady" and that still causes him to experience "sudden bouts of shame" decades later. The listless state of the child in the pew —an early manifestation of *ennui*— made him an "outcast" from the rituals of piety and communion. And who knows, maybe all waiting contains the seeds of such exclusion. For even when we are waiting in the company of others, each of us is actually waiting alone. Like sleep, waiting cannot be shared—by playing games or telling stories, for instance; it can only be outsmarted individually. Isn't it precisely this insight that animates the plot of *Arabian Nights*—that classical tale of deferral in which a vizier's daughter succeeds in staying her execution by regaling the king with an artfully crafted set of tales that she continually interrupts at the most exciting moment?

King Shahryar, having become a staunch misogynist after his first wife's infidelity, takes a new virgin to bed every night only to have her beheaded in the morning. The same fate awaits the beautiful Scheherazade. By telling the king a story every night, which she promises to continue the next day, however, she manages to delay her beheading. After one thousand and one nights, she presents the king with the three sons that have been born to him in the meantime, and the king, bewitched by her narrative, takes her as his wife.

This kind of happy ending is certainly not something that anybody sentenced to death can typically count on. What makes waiting for one's execution presumably so horribly excruciating is the overwhelming loneliness that goes along with it—a loneliness emblematically captured in the passion of Christ. Hardly any other episode illuminates the twofold abyss of anxiety and loneliness as profoundly as that of Jesus and his disciples in the Garden of Gethsemane: "Then cometh Jesus with them unto a place called Gethsemane, and saith unto the disciples, 'Sit ye here, while I go and pray yonder'. And he took with him Peter and the two sons of Zebedee, and began to be sorrowful and very heavy. Then saith he unto them, 'My soul is exceeding sorrowful, even unto death: tarry ye here, and watch with me'. And he went a little further, and fell on his face, and prayed, saying, 'O my Father, if it be possible, let this cup pass from me: nevertheless, not as I will, but as thou *wilt*'. And he cometh unto the disciples, and findeth them asleep, and saith unto Peter, 'What, could ye not watch with me one hour? Watch and pray, that ye enter not into temptation: the spirit indeed is willing, but the flesh is weak'." Three times Jesus finds his disciples, who are supposed to wake with him, overcome by sleep, until, finally, "came they, and laid hands on Jesus, and took him."

Owing to the expectation of his imminent resurrection, the ultimate deadline Jesus faces will have always already been translated into a temporal dimension that cannot be accounted for in worldly time. Yet, the life and teaching of Jesus the man are inexorably ruled by the dictate of this life's brevity. "When Jesus begins his ministry at the age of thirty," cultural critic Harald Weinrich observes, "he places his gospel from the very start under the sign of an inevitable decision that brooks no delay." So little time, in fact, does the Son of Man have that he even subjects prayer to an *economy of time conservation* and presents his teachings in short, memorable parables.

The inner turmoil into which an impending execution will throw a person can hardly be captured with abstract concepts, Weinrich continues: "Here, only narrative, drawn from real or fictive sources, can provide reliable information … It may not only give us an intimate sense of what it means to live with such deadlines, but, at times, even save us from them."

To prolong the grace period of our existence in the face of mortality is, as Proust famously put it, "the cruel law of art." The wish to while away our allotted time in the company of others might be the root of all narrative, which, in turn, in its myriad permutations, might be but the expression of the very essence of waiting. In their desire to hear the same stories over and over again—as if such repetition could ensure that life quietly and reliably go on and on—children intuitively tap into the experience of time embedded in ancient lore. It almost seems as though our culture of endless entertainment were a disenchanted, belated iteration of *Arabian Nights*, and the latter a prelude to our daytime soaps, whose episodes always leave us dying to know what happens next. But should TV indeed turn out to be our own latter-day Scheherazade, then we have certainly no happy ending to which to look forward.

Not Now

"Keeping others waiting," Roland Barthes remarks, "is the prerogative of the powerful." Executive suites are filled with people who arrogate and greedily consume our time. Whoever makes us wait celebrates his power over our lives, and what's especially threatening about it is that we can never be sure that we aren't made to wait for precisely this reason.

Since time immemorial, curtailing another's freedom of movement, making him stay put, has been a patriarchal privilege; and, as the story of the Fall demonstrates, disobeying the powers that be may entail severe consequences. Even today, whenever we *have to* wait for someone, we sometimes can't shake the feeling that if we happen to leave too soon we may have to pay for it, if only by burning bridges we didn't mean to burn, or, in the worst case, by not being allowed back.

Captivity, in all its forms, too, is defined by the loss of the freedom to choose the spaces one would inhabit and the rhythms by which one would live. Thus, as Michel Foucault has shown, in the totalitarian world of prisons, where constant surveillance and rigid discipline strip the inmate down to the last second and twitch, even the light switch obeys the authorities. Could this be the reason that in war, where waiting for the right moment is of utmost strategic importance and long periods are spent in anxious expectation, the one who decides to leave early, the deserter, must pay for it with his life?

Being sentenced to waiting is a curse, and whoever puts it on us has us in his grip. A person or institution forces a rhythm of being upon us that goes against our own fundamental sense of lived time, and that's what makes this situation so depressing. Waiting is impotence, and the fact that we might not be able to get out of this predicament on our own is a humiliation that skews our perception of the world as a whole—which is why the one waiting often feels that he has been wronged, that he is being penalized for no reason. The passivity of waiting, the sense of condemnation that often goes along with it, can almost feel like corporal punishment, being both shameful and painful.

There's a reason that the arbitrary authority of bureaucracies has come to epitomize the torture of waiting as well as the brutality of dictatorships at large. The government agency is the quintessential modern waiting room. There, the meaninglessness of waiting penetrates every fiber of those waiting. Cultural critic Siegfried Kracauer has captured the demoralizing effects of public waiting areas in his observations on the goings-on at the Berlin Department of Labor during the Great Depression: "Here poverty constantly looks itself in the face—making itself at home in stained, dirty rags, or bashfully withdrawing into middle-class shame … If it succeeds in veiling itself in one place, it will soon expose itself in another … Those waiting must bear a twofold burden in each other's cruel company. They seek to distract themselves in any way possible, but whatever they do, they cannot shake the meaninglessness of it all … The older ones may succeed in resigning themselves to waiting as if to an old comrade; for the younger ones who are out of work, however, it is a poison that gradually eats them up."

Certainly, the situation of today's unemployed is different from the situation in the 1930s; but what hasn't changed is the very air or feel of uniform public waiting areas, which still reflect reigning social conditions. Kracauer called them "society's dreams," believing that if we learn to decipher them properly the "foundations of social reality" will be laid bare, and all that has been swept under the rug or suppressed will suddenly come to light.

Government agencies always feel like correctional facilities designed to discipline and punish: scuffed furnishings, stark neon lights, numbers that assign everyone an exact spot in line, the unmistakable air of supplication. The architecture—inherently depressing to petitioners of all colors—echoes the dismal realities of transition and refugee camps, where waiting for a brighter future often turns into a limbo between exile and deportation. And although the harsh realities of persecution and flight have no place amidst the bland, impersonal trappings of First-World societies, the memory of the long history of bureaucratic stalling is ever present whenever we happen to stand in line in linoleum-lined hallways: the heart and soul, the dark essence of waiting.

Kafka has given us the most memorable metaphor for the encroachment of bureaucracy upon our lives: insurance agent Gregor Samsa's notorious metamorphosis into a "monstrous vermin." Just how massively the nightmare of time gratuitously killed in the mazes of bureaucracy has taken hold of the individual comes to the fore most hauntingly in Gregor's horror at finding himself literally possessed one morning. This prototypical allegory of the modern age is the exact opposite of Proust's dreamy quest for "lost time." Kafka's novella *The Metamorphosis* and Proust's novel *In Search of Lost Time* are the points of departure for two radically distinct cultural projects: the one wholly devoted to the past, the other wholly resigned to the futility of past, present, and future. Proust and Kafka are the crown witnesses to our world's transition into the age of accelerated time; and Kafka, for one, was the first to put the total administration of humanity on trial. The man who wasted his life waiting in front of the "gate of the Law" in Kafka's novel *The Trial* —prevented from entering by a low-level official (or his own lack of courage)—is anxious modern man *par excellence*:

Before the Law stands a gatekeeper. To this gatekeeper there comes a countryman and requests entry to the Law. But the gate-keeper says that he cannot grant him entry just now. The man ponders this and asks if he will be allowed in later. 'It's possible', says the gatekeeper, 'but not now'. Since the gate to the Law is open as usual, and the gatekeeper steps to the side, the man stoops to peer inside through the gate. Noticing this, the gatekeeper laughs: 'If you want it so badly, just try to get in against my ex-press orders. But remember, I am powerful, and I am only the lowest of the gatekeepers. There will be gatekeepers in every hall, each more powerful than the last. The third one already is so terrible that even I can't bear looking at him'. The countryman did not expect such difficulties; surely, the Law ought to be accessible to all at all times; but as he now takes a closer look at the gate-keeper in his fur coat, with his big, pointy nose and long, thin, black Tartar beard, he decides that he'd better wait until he is al-lowed in. The gatekeeper gives him a stool and lets him sit down on one side of the gate. There he sits for days and years.

The gatekeeper, who soon becomes the coun-tryman's sole focus, is the fallen angel blocking the way back into Proust's bourgeois paradise: "The man, who has brought many provisions along," Kafka continues, "uses everything, however valuable, to bribe the gatekeeper. And while the latter accepts everything, he always says: 'I only accept it so as to make sure that you don't think you haven't tried everything'." As the years go by, the countryman "forgets about the other gatekeepers, and this, first one, appears to him as the only obstacle to his entry into the Law." Eventually, his "eyesight begins to fail," yet all the while he can still clearly see the "light emanating inextinguishably from the gate of the Law." Shortly before he dies, his "experiences over the years" contract into one, final question: "Isn't it true that everyone strives for the Law?" he asks the gatekeeper. "How come, then, that in all these years no one else has requested entry to it?" To which the gatekeeper responds: "Nobody else could have been granted entry here, for this gate was made for you alone. Now I will go and close it."

This parable poignantly stages the bleak circularity of a waiting consumed with itself. Like the heroes of Kafka's inscrutable stories and novels we all see the light in the distance but don't dare to follow it because the many insignificant obstacles we encounter along the way appear to us as insurmountable as the gatekeeper to Kafka's countryman. Only when it's already too late might the one who has spent a lifetime waiting realize: "This gate was made for you alone." Or, in Robert Lowell's pithy words that sum up the dilemma of waiting too long: "If we see the light at the end of the tunnel, it's the light of the oncoming train."

A Little Conversation

> They give birth astride of a grave, the
> light gleams an instant, then it's night
> once more.
>
> (Samuel Beckett)

It's only a small step from tragedy to comedy,
and Samuel Beckett took this step for all of
us. "The entire time he'd been waiting," reads
an entry in one of Beckett's working note-
books, "waiting itself was his destiny—and
that's the whole awful truth." It fell to Beckett to write the ending to Kafka's parable.
Beckett's heroes are the modern descendants
of Sisyphus—famously condemned to his exercise in futility for outsmarting death—and
Godot is the new name for the rock they roll
up the mountain during the day and see tum-
bling down again during the night, when they
put off waiting "until tomorrow." Yet, as Albert Camus suggested—anticipating Beckett's *Waiting for Godot*, in which the incest-
uousness of waiting is but a metaphor for the
absurdity of existence—one must imagine
Sisyphus happy. "That passed the time,"

Vladimir, one of the characters in *Waiting for Godot*, observes. "It would have passed in any case," Estragon, his interlocutor, replies. And so, in the face of the existential void they are in, the play's protagonists resort to what most of us do most of the time: "a little conversation."

Beckett's down-and-out characters, caught in infinite loops of drawn-out monologue, practice waiting for its own sake and with no particular goal in mind. Severed from all social networks that give life direction and meaning, they are suspended between an empty heaven and an open grave. The worst that can happen to them are breaks, and their "end- games" are all designed to get them through these breaks—that's what makes them poetic.

In August 1984, Hungarian playwright George Tabori went to Paris to meet with Samuel Beckett. In his essay *Waiting for Beckett*, he describes how he spent half a day and one night in expectation of the master: "'They also serve who only stand and wait'. Equipped with this kind of Miltonian humility, I arrived twelve hours early just to make sure that I wouldn't miss our appointment. Beckett, in turn, arrived sixty-three seconds late. To me, this felt like a most appropriate exercise in what Beckett's play is supposedly all about, if, that is, that's what it's actually about ... After all, 'nothing is certain', as Estragon says."

Thus, if *Waiting for Godot* can indeed be said to be about waiting, it's in the sense that waiting and enduring are one and the same. But you never know. Beckett's texts attest to the bankruptcy of all eschatology. It could also be, Tabori suggests, that "*Waiting for Godot* is the first genuine religious farce; it shows the funny side of religion, rather than making fun of it."

Tabori's interpretation of Beckett's "crepuscular play" is probably one of the most insightful, insofar as it discloses, in the sustained (if unfulfilled) hope, that Godot might show up in the end, the theatrical dimension of all waiting—for isn't theater essentially pure expectation? "Theater always means waiting for 'it' to happen. As spectators, we wait for the bad guy to be punished, for the lovers to reunite, for the king's messenger to arrive in time." Beckett's great innovation, according to Tabori, consists precisely in refusing to "let 'it' happen." Contrary to all prophets of hopelessness, however, Godot's absence is far from tragic—in fact, it's quite a stroke of good luck. For as long as we have something to wait for, our life has a purpose. It's all about the return of the ideal spectator, night after night, who willingly accepts the same challenge as Beckett's characters Vladimir and Estragon: "So long as we show up at the appointed hour we'll be saved; if we come late, we'll be punished— Christian dramaturgy 101: life waits for life to begin after it ends."

In a way, then, *Waiting for Godot* can be said to be "the best Christian play since Bach's *St. Matthew Passion*—passion as vaudeville and love story." For Godot will not be coming tonight, most probably tomorrow, though. Tabori always believed that, and that's why he "never minded that Godot never came." Vladimir and Estragon, meanwhile, ought to be viewed as lovers at heart. "As long as they meet at night their love is whole—and that's what we all should worry about: love's wholeness." Which means: the one waiting wants to be saved from waiting as little as the lover from love.

Beckett's parodistic attempt to do away (thereby dashing any hope of redemption once and for all) with "the existence ... of a personal God ... outside time without extension who from the heights of divine apathia ... loves us dearly with some exceptions for reasons unknown ...," is part and parcel of the logic of a waiting that contains nothing but waiting itself. Time, after all, would have passed in any case.

Felt Time

Waiting structurally implies the possibility that it might never end, which doesn't mean, however, that it can't also have definite boundaries, as between two scheduled events: at such and such a time, one event will end, and at such and such a time another event is slated to begin—nothing to do but kill time, withdraw into ourselves, read, or have a cup of coffee and a cigarette. Think of all the moments when we'd light up, or ask someone for a light—frivolously wasted time, dissipated in blue nicotine fog. This flirtatious ritual—becoming the lone wolf as much as his blasé female counterpart—is but a fading memory of how we used to spend our breaks in the last century; and those few huddled types who still engage in it must freeze it out on balconies or outside office buildings.

With or without smoke—nobody can possibly know how long waiting feels to the one actually doing the waiting. The duration of waiting is completely subjective. No sooner is the flow of the foreseeable interrupted than we immediately turn into wild cats awaiting their feeding. In the best case, waiting is a gift of time; more often than not, it's simply time lost—always, however, it makes time itself palpable.

Whenever we do something productive or set out to accomplish certain goals while waiting for someone to arrive or something to happen, an element of gamesmanship comes into play allowing us to experience the very tediousness of waiting as a kind of moral victory over ourselves. We might even derive great pleasure from succeeding in rewriting the *curse of having to wait as the blessing of choosing to take a break*. Aren't most of our lives built around such structures of self-deception that help us to gloss over the *horror vacui?*

At the Doctor's

Waiting feels particularly aggravating when illness-related. Thus, for the one anxiously waiting for a diagnosis, time itself is but a stay of execution and the waiting room at the doctor's office a limbo where, in the company of others, he burns in the hell of uncertainty. Maybe that's why all waiting rooms resemble each other: the line-up of chairs, furnishings, and magazines; the play areas for children with their obligatory picture books, toy trains, and building blocks; the Van Gogh, Renoir, and O'Keefe prints on the walls— the whole nine yards of inexpensive decor designed to make us feel good and equally characteristic of hospitals and cheap hotels. As if, in these depersonalized spaces, the experience of waiting, too, must be stripped of all individuality in the name of uniformity.

But the anonymity of waiting rooms is also a protection mechanism: the tension-filled proximity of the patiently enduring requires the counterweight of a neutral ambiance. Isn't it strange how, in a doctor's waiting room, we join a community of fate? Our ills seem to resemble each other just like the chairs we sit on: we are all *patients*—a word that already contains *patience*. We are all here for the same reason. Yet, amidst this compulsory intimacy, we quickly register differences. The first thing we notice is that some people are doing worse than others. Waiting quickly turns into the study of tics, clothing, and other idiosyncrasies. That woman over there could be right out of Vermeer—just imagine her with a bonnet and stay. She probably works at a bank, leaves home early every day, and dreams about Leonardo di Caprio; or the short-cropped guy over there who scratches himself all the time—he looks a little like Brad Pitt but doesn't seem to know how much better-looking he could be if only he had a little bit more self-discipline ... Already we have begun sketching biographies that might fit the faces in the crowd—after all, focusing on the lives of others makes the burden of our own condition easier to bear, for a while anyway.

If it's true, as mind-body expert Georg Grodeck has suggested, that every illness is also a way of protecting oneself against a more severe illness, then it would make sense to view illness as the body's way of taking a break from its total functionalization within the fast-paced machinery of regulated time. For, at bottom, falling ill puts us into a state of waiting in which we are confronted with the specific retardations of our physical being. Illness partakes of two registers of temporality: the sheer *presence* of being ill, and the *anticipation* of convalescence—that wholesome experience of physical exhaustion coupled with the invigorating expectation of being gently returned to the world of obligation and duty, which brings back childhood memories of recovering under the loving care of adults, when, within a bubble of unregulated, reading-filled, bed-ridden time, we felt safe from the encroachment of the mundane.

Where waiting is accompanied by pain—as in the emergency room, for instance—it shows its true feral nature. When we anxiously hope for pain relief, the power others have over us is revealed in the most brutal way. If there were an angel of waiting, he would surely be an anesthesiologist. As soon as anesthesia plunges us into oblivion, waiting becomes someone else's problem. Now, *they* have to wait for us to come to again. Unawares, *they* have been saddled with a part of *our* life that will have transpired without us. As we come out of anesthesia, we yet again realize that living always means reckoning with death. But the opposite is also true. A devastating diagnosis can have the effect of making us wish to cheat the time that remains by cramming it with as many experiences as possible, especially of things we haven't done yet but always wanted to do and that *can no longer wait*—as if they had always been sitting there for the taking. But, as anyone who has ever tried it knows: catching up on things left undone is easier said than done. Caerus doesn't like to be pressed, and trying to seize him by his tuft of hair we find out soon enough that he may be wearing a wig. Opportunities missed, too, had their moment.

Interlude

Expectation, Plundered Time

For a long time I used to spend afternoons in cafés. I would sit there for hours pretending to read the paper and never making it past the headlines. I still remember the rain tapping on the windows, and the background bustle of dinner rush. I'd wait, a cup of coffee before me, behind me the ghosts of hours wasted. Anxiousness —I could have invented it—that unspecified longing, indistinguishable from fear. Uselessness, plundered days. I'd been forgotten by something, I'd missed something. At such moments, I longed to be back in a past that belonged to someone else, before my time. But it seems that, come what may, in the end we'll always have fallen behind our longings.

3. HESITATION

Limping Days

Illness often plunges us into boredom. Life turns into a gooey mass of time that feels like "the void of the heart in the face of empty time," as Romanian philosopher Emil Cioran once described the experience of *ennui*. Today, this state would most likely be diagnosed as clinical depression. It sets in when we no longer remember what we've been waiting for, and the only thing we are aware of in its void is the throbbing of time itself.

Once upon a time, this languor gave birth to libraries full of dark reflection, and it has always been a gold mine for literature. "Nothing is as tedious as those limping days / When under the heavy flakes of snowed-in years / Boredom, the fruit of glum incuriosity, / Takes on the proportions of immortality," Charles Baudelaire wrote in *The Flowers of Evil*—that book of verse in which the flowers of the poetic moment were picked on the sides of the *grands boulevards*. He first introduced the turtle as pacemaker into nineteenth-century Paris; it served the bohemians of the day as a welcome contrast to the frenzy of industrial acceleration and set the time signatures for the Paris arcades. But even before the dandy made *ennui* a social staple, it had long been the devil's playing field; here, particularly in the age of *Dangerous Liaisons*, rakes, cads, and roués would congregate, and literature led the way.

"Since the first novel that she secretly read at the age of fifteen," Stendhal remarked, "a woman quietly pines away for passionate love." Gustave Flaubert's *Madame Bovary* was to become the epitome of this kind of longing for erotic fulfillment feeding on boredom and literature: "Her life was as empty and cold as a granary with northern exposure, and boredom, like an ugly spider, was weaving its web in the corners of her heart … She was waiting for something to happen, like a sailor in distress, anxiously scanning the bleak horizon of her life for a distant lodestar …"

—which was indeed about to appear in the guise of one Rodolphe.

It goes without saying that female resistance to this kind of imposed lifelong waiting was bound to lead to disaster, especially when compounded by missed deadlines. Emma Bovary's addiction to cosmetics and fashion—a proven method for coping with depression to this day—is the prelude to the punishment awaiting all adulteresses in the nineteenth century, after their affairs tapered off under society's pressures. Emma's creditor, no longer willing to wait for his payments, drives her to suicide—a way out that Emma's literary sisters Effi Briest and Anna Karenina will also take. Only in the second half of the twentieth century would women finally be released from the prison of languishing expectation they had been confined to in the name of nature. But dreaming about Prince Charming is still a fantasy that many seem to buy into—at least according to the collective myths propagated by the tabloids.

Interlude

The Sleeping Muse

I know she cannot be summoned, her sleep cannot be disturbed—in that she's eternal. And yet, off and on, she does visit. And so I wait for her, try to bait her with the undulations of idleness, offer her all manner of baubles. But, no, she cannot be tempted. I must forget her for her to dream of me and be awakened by jealousy.

Hesitation Before Birth

Cultural critic Walter Benjamin called boredom "the dream bird that hatches the egg of experience." In other words, boredom can be a holding pattern, a time of inner gathering and preparation. In the same vein, memoirist Dieter Wellershoff has suggested that "boredom—not the pathological kind but that intermittent mood marking periods of growth —shuts the world out only to let it in again; it disturbs the peaceful coexistence the world and I may have settled into and infuses life with a renewed sense of wonder that makes the paralysis of the soul it caused initially suddenly turn into its opposite, into a sense of unspecified expectation—which may actually not be the opposite at all but rather its very apogee, the flooding of life into the spaces vacated by waiting."

This description hearkens back to Nietzsche's notion of the "windless calm of the soul," which "precedes the happy voyage and the pleasant winds" and which no creative person can possibly avoid "*waiting for* to take effect in him"—something that, according to Nietzsche, "only very few know how to do." Or, in more contemporary terms: something that we no longer plan or have the time for in the age of *permanent gratification compulsion*. Yet, it is precisely in this state of patient *awaiting* that we are able to cast our nets wide into the waters of oblivion and make a catch—for in the lee of the soul's "windless calm" the great idea lies in wait.

Distraction, too, is part and parcel of the creative effort. All those evasion maneuvers —like doing chores around the house only

to avoid anxiously staring at the blank page
—serve both as a way of relaxation *and* ten-
sion-building: something is brewing within
us, our thoughts need a little more time in
order to gather and present themselves in the
right order.

Nobody has probed the affinity between
writing and waiting as painstakingly as Kafka.
According to his own testimony, he experienced the state of creative anticipation as a
"hesitation before birth." You have to picture
him carrying out his "devil's service" to the
muses in the furthest-most cell of an under-
ground dungeon—at least that's how he envisioned his ideal workplace; once every
night someone would deliver a frugal meal
to his door with a gentle knock, and go away
again.

The motif of waiting pervades Kafka's
novels and stories like a persistent irritation.
In the world of Kafka, whose entire oeuvre
is predicated on the inversion of waking and
sleeping, night reigned supreme. That he
himself had actually ever experienced restful,
recuperative sleep is probably hard to imag-

ine, although he didn't seem to feel that way at all. As this unhappy insurance agent avowed, while his nights may have been spent in "dubious embraces" with the dark powers of the imagination, his days were punctuated by extended periods during which he'd be "more asleep talking and dictating than when actually sleeping."

The somnambulist's self-forgetting that Kafka strove for as the condition for writing resembles the dream state in which the patterns of the unconscious gradually appear on the soul's matrix. Yet while dreams arbitrarily paint the chambers of sleep with our fears and desires, the actual rendezvous with the muses tends to be a somewhat more sober, 'chaperoned' affair. As much as literature—poetry in particular—may at times appear to be the product of trance, which ostensibly dictates its images to writing's daydreams, it is only in the liminal state *between* sleeping and waking, when consciousness is no longer anesthetized nor yet wholly ruled by reason, that dreams yield their metaphorical surplus value. Authors are threshold experts, interpreting between inner and outer worlds, constructing their sentences by fusing memory and thought, method and meditation, grammar and imagery. Art, it has been said, consists of ten percent inspiration and ninety percent perspiration. And without the rift in time that allows the muse to alight on our doorstep all labors are in vain. But the muse will not be pressured. All we can do is prepare for her visit and wait.

Biding Our Time

Waiting and expecting are not quite the same. Expectation is more on the side of the *future*, while waiting—as lived duration—is, paradoxically, more on the side of the *present*. When we *expect*, we are typically transported into the imminent future of whatever it is we expect to happen—if not right away, then at least very soon. When we *wait*, on the other hand, we tend to abide in a state of continued (if future-oriented) *presence*, looking ahead to a time when whatever it is we are concerned with *at the moment* might be over (which may never happen).

Waiting for the right moment, the cue, the split-second when our instincts tell us *now!* is probably one of the most important skills one can possibly learn. It requires chance and a stroke of good luck for a "person in whom the solution to a problem lies dormant to kick into action in time," Nietzsche wrote. More often than not, however, "this doesn't happen, and the world is full of people who neither know what they are waiting for nor that they are actually waiting in vain." Every action depends on the right moment, and it can always happen that its "wake-up call"—the accident that becomes its catalyst—comes too late and "we let our youth and energy go to waste by doing nothing." For whenever waiting turns into dithering, Mephistopheles' warning to Faust still applies: "Letting the right moment to act go by, / you call letting things unfold on their own time." Appositely, in Dante's *Inferno* the eternally dithering must suffer in limbo for as long as their squandered lives lasted—unless, that is, they are saved by the pious.

Every conspiracy, every act of revenge, too, pivots on the ability to wait—the God of wrath has put the buffer of hesitation between the convulsions of hatred and the execution of revenge. This means that waiting entails guilt. From the initial flaring up of emotion, to conscious intent, to actually planning the deed, our temperature drops to the freeze point of cold-blooded premeditation, when strategy and ruse finally begin to pay off. "The person driven by thoughts of revenge," philosopher Peter Sloterdijk has observed, "emphatically knows what it means to have a plan"; biding his time, "he makes history, insofar as *making* here implies drawing from the wells of the past the motives for taking care of the future—in this respect, nothing compares with revenge."

Biding our time in anxious expectation rather than jumping the gun also harbors the promise of happiness: it's the real manifestation of hope. When we're all excitement and expectation, it's as if we've momentarily lost consciousness. Like the dog that stubbornly anticipates the next bite with every bite withheld, expectation doesn't learn from the past. I can stubbornly expect something that reason tells me will definitely not happen, or I can know exactly when my waiting is supposed to be over and still wish to speed things along. This animal obstinacy of the heart is incorrigible: I'm waiting for a letter, I know that the other won't write or call before such and such a date and time; and yet, I check, over and over again, if perhaps a kindly spirit hasn't foiled his plans and heard my prayers.

Interlude

Keeping the Other Waiting

I'm late, again. In this case, the other's waiting and expecting are one. I know he expects me to call in case I'm running late. I see him before me, scanning the room. He expects me to enter any minute now. He checks his watch, gets impatient at first, then restless, then worried (for a split-second—

that's my consolation, my triumph), and, finally, angry. Now the mood will be spoiled when I arrive. I have to be careful not to remind him that last time he was the one who'd kept me waiting. When we keep the other waiting only the 'now' counts. This one time being late renders all other instances of tardiness and punctuality meaningless. Still, whether I'd intended it or not, I've won a small victory over his desire to see me enter eventually—if only finally to put an end to waiting.

Messengers of Death

From your letter today I gather what you must have gone through yesterday. As always, I mailed my registered letter before 5pm the day before yesterday. Tomorrow's letter from you will probably inform me that my letter has arrived in the meantime, just as your letter today tells me that my earlier letter … has finally reached you … It must have taken twenty-six hours for it to get to you, and the registered letter I mailed the day before yesterday seems to be taking as long, if not longer. Please let me know when exactly you've received it so I can file a complaint. I'm afraid that yesterday's and to- day's letters will be delayed as well, or maybe all three will arrive at the same time. (By the way, I've been reimbursed for the telegram that was never delivered.) Living in this country has become impossible.

(Karl Kraus, in a letter to
Sidonie von Nadherny)

Since the invention of mail, waiting for a letter has symbolized unquenchable longing. A letter always embodies the distance it must travel by coach, boat, train, or plane. The age of letter-writing was above all an age of delays. Even a letter's tactile quality (from the handwritten or printed sheets to the envelope that turns every missive into a potential secret agent entrusted with classified information) is of the very essence of its journey through time and space. We still recognize— today more than ever perhaps—the preciousness of such freight rife with human destiny and suffused with the presence of the one who wrote it. Could this be the reason that junk mail often simulates the handwritten address on the envelope? All this, however, will soon be a thing of the past. In the digital age, the rhythms of personal interaction have adapted to high-speed online communication and, thus, to virtual simultaneity. Yet our accelerated modes of exchange have not brought relief from the pain of waiting. In fact, the promise of the virtually instant fulfillment of our digitally synchronized expectations and desires has only exacerbated our impatience. That's especially true of all communication concerning matters of the heart. Not only do we now expect immediate replies to our e-mails and texts, but we even curse the time it takes to write them.

Certainly, the simulation of simultaneity and presence has always been the goal of sentimental letter-writing. Take Goethe for instance, who, in his correspondence with Augusta von Stolberg, composed a veritable book of hours in which he meticulously recorded his daily routine, thus allowing his interlocutor to participate in all his thoughts and activities as if in real time: "... had a good morning after a good night's sleep and feel like a wench …You couldn't possibly divine what's on my mind: the mask I shall wear at the ball on Tuesday … after lunch: am in a hurry to tell you what's on my mind: no other woman loves me as much as my Augusta … half past three—fell into the well—I'd feared this might happen … half past four—I wish I could show myself to you as I am …"

We seem to have come awfully close to realizing Goethe's dream of immediate presence and authenticity. For even though it's completely devoid of anything physical or sensual, electronic communication actually expands the zones of intimacy. Its leisurely forms of address, which oscillate between the written and the oral, allow for a particular kind of openness and familiarity between people who wouldn't necessarily get along in person. The bashful lose their inhibitions, the rhetorically clumsy rise to the heights of verbal finesse. The web's imaginary spaces, where the doubts of waiting give way to virtual certainty, relieve us of the weight of existence with all its practical defects. Even among complete strangers all speech registers are suddenly permitted—the *mailbox* is a space of intimacy without essence, everything in it remains provisional. Maybe that's why so many love stories begin on the Internet nowadays—after all, nothing resembles the first rush of a crush so much as the purely imaginary character of an e-mail romance.

What happens if words are stripped of their journeys, of the distances that allow them to accrue meanings we may not have had in mind when we wrote them? Don't they lose a whole range of possible readings? Doesn't mailing a letter imply reaching into the future—the future of the journey inscribed in it, the future of its arrival in the hands of the recipient we had envisioned, and, most importantly, the future of the range of unanticipated interpretations and surprises that we may have initiated, yet not at all intended, by writing it?

The time between mailing and receiving a letter can often be the source of miscommunication and great confusion:

February 2, 1970
Paul, dearest,
the days are rife with strife—on all sides—
with myself, the hours, the minutes, the
mailbox—with you and for you—they are
filled with waiting … For how long? For
what?

Addressing these desperate lines to Paul
Celan, Ilana Schmueli must have anticipated
that her friendship with the poet was about
to take a dark turn. On April 12, 1970, Celan
wrote his last letter to her: "Don't worry if
you don't receive a letter from me for a
while—eight or ten days; as of tomorrow
the postal services will be on strike." Paul
Celan committed suicide on April 19, 1970.

It's no coincidence that the poet factored
the unreliability of mail into his final calcu-
lation by way of allaying the worries of his
friend in Israel. For the time it may take a letter to reach its destination has always been a
seedbed of anxiety and chagrin—especially
when it arrives too late or not at all. "Letters
that arrive too late are messengers of death,"
Charlotte von Kalb wrote to her tardy cor-

respondent, novelist Jean Paul Richter. Many a play—comedies and tragedies alike—is predicated on this maddening aspect of epistolary communication, due in large part to the unreliability of messengers. Take *Romeo and Juliet* for instance, the prototypical tragedy of missed letters, in which two lovers who are literally dying to be together actually have to die to achieve their goal, the victims of a tardy messenger. Delayed letters are messengers of death indeed—if only the death of our expectations, which may have changed course in the meantime. And although, as cultural critic Manfred Schneider observes, modern technology—from the telephone to the Internet—has certainly provided a convenient outlet for our erstwhile "postal paranoia," thus in no small part contributing to the world's becoming ever more *rational*, the "phantoms, ghosts, vampires, and elemental spirits of the past" continue to haunt our technological innovations, and nobody knows exactly where they might be lying in wait.

Time Is Money

> We speak of waiting when there is
> more than enough time, yet time itself
> doesn't have enough of it. This over-
> abundance of too little time is the per-
> manent condition of waiting.
>
> (Maurice Blanchot)

Insofar as it is conceived of as the age of mobility, modernity can also be described as the
era of shortened wait times. Technology is
constantly working toward eliminating the
times and spaces *between*. The creation of
speed as we know it began with the Industrial
Revolution; since then, life has been meas-
ured for the most part in strictly secular
time. We have evolved into slaves in a global
economy of acceleration, and have come to
view life in terms of a tight budget that we
constantly rebalance with the daily help of
our crammed planners, PDAs, iPhones, and
other gadgets that, ideally, mustn't contain
the blemish of even a single scheduling gap.
When time itself is experienced as delay, we
know that we suffer from *efficiency compul-*

sion—also known as the *time-is-money-syn-drome*—which hinges on the paradox that with every saved chunk of time the time deficit grows as well.

The time we may be objectively saving courtesy of the *age of acceleration* reveals itself, against the foil of the time signatures of the new technologies and forms of communication, as a waste of both time and money. Ironically, though, while the distances may be shrinking, the spaces contracting, and the units of measurable time dwindling, the lines in our mobile societies are getting longer and longer; whether in government agencies or cellular holding patterns—our basic experience is one of time wasted. Dead eternities at railroad stations, airports, and the call centers of life: "please, wait" is the mantra of the new rhetoric of appeasement, the synthetic global muzak that has made patience *the* cardinal virtue of service-based societies.

At the Train Station

When I looked at my watch at 10:30
it was still 9:30.

(Alfred Polgar)

Philosopher Martin Heidegger once took the
experience of waiting for a train as a point of
departure for reflecting on the possibility of
"conjuring away boredom by rushing time itself." Think of a "tiny, inconspicuous regional
train station" as dull as the surrounding land-
scape. The next train isn't due for another
four hours; impossible to read or "think
through a problem," and even the repeated
perusal of the timetables doesn't help in
terms of speeding things along—and so we
take to the street, "count the trees, check our
watches—not more than five minutes have
passed since we last checked …" This would
go on and on, Heidegger remarks, if we had-
n't learned *how* to wait *properly*, namely, in
the manner of "waiting as letting it be …
waiting as meditation." For only the one who
knows how to let himself fall into waiting

(that is, into his very being) can expect the train to arrive at all (if indeed it ever comes).

In a non-metaphysical sense, of course, waiting for a train always follows a schedule that measures our inner tension down to the last second. The public address system scans the rhythms of our impatience, which sets in with the very first delay, which will entail missing a connection, which will entail missing an appointment, which will lead to yet another missed opportunity … All timing, after all, depends on the punctuality of our means of transportation and their dependable coordination. Ironically, where everything is geared precisely toward eliminating wait times and going according to plan, time unplanned creeps in through the back door. With the first cracking noises from the loudspeakers, which are immediately followed by the dreaded announcement that "the train has been delayed," those waiting on the platform are joined in a community of anger. Suddenly, we all begin to act in a similar way, no longer able to keep still. The clock of collective impatience has issued the marching orders for a restless to and fro. Inevitably, some of us will begin complaining and grumbling, or demonstratively pacing back and forth, checking the displays and clocks—all that wasted energy! Anger is never as conformist as when we feel we've been cheated, misled, duped by our own foolish expectations. And what better way to vent than to rail at the railroad system's unreliability. Perhaps our impatience with tardiness in general (stoked as it might be by the Protestant ethos) is a function of timetables, which first allowed us to experience duration collectively.

Timetables are only two hundred years old. In the early days of European transportation only the departure and arrival dates would be announced. Well into the nineteenth century, timetables were taken seriously so little that satirist Ludwig Börne felt compelled to compose a "doctrine of the standstill of coaches" and to deride (in a typically self-deprecating German way) the "quiescent" introspection of Germans, who are "utterly devoid of derring-do." Indeed, while the French for instance had always been much faster at most things, in the German Reich the clocks would not be set to Central European Time and the timetables for stage coaches not adjusted accordingly until 1893.

It all began with the steam engine, which first set modernity on its high-speed course. "The railroad kills space, and what remains is pure time," Heinrich Heine wrote from Paris in 1843; "I feel as though all the forests and mountains were advancing on Paris. I can already smell the fragrance of German lime trees, and at my doorstep the North Sea is roaring." That was when the railroad was barely eighteen years old. Since then, space has contracted even further, and the seas roar everywhere. Airports cater to humankind's desire for travel so comprehensively that the very notion of *wanderlust*—stemming from the age of Romantic longing when venturing forth meant maturing, and whoever went away returned a different person—has become an anachronism.

4. EXPECTATION

Interlude

Always Homeward Bound

Even before we arrive we have covered great distances ... Isn't longing essentially tied to water? The waves' heartbeat, rhythm, and roar restore the body that first carried us through space. Where we come from, where we're going—these 'last questions' arise time and again when we travel. The fact that it may have shadowed humankind since Odysseus first set out to sea doesn't make the motif of life's journey trivial in any way. Embarking, departing, and making landfall on foreign shores is one of our deepest longings—our tourist's jadedness notwithstanding; it hails from Eden, and it's supposed to lead us back there. Traveling means jump-cutting through time, on the trail of our oldest anxiety, which associates leaving and coming back with the danger of not being recognized upon our return (like Odysseus). But every grand departure also promises the triumph of first being prop-

erly valued (like the Prodigal Son). That's why trav-
eling implies someone waiting for us at home and
acknowledging our return.

Eros Is Transitory

You have to travel by boat or plane to step onto new soil for the first time. The feeling of literally losing one's footing for the duration of a flight or cruise makes us first truly open to the new, and the sense of magic associated with arriving on foreign shores may in no small part be due to a change in elements. The image of New York's skyline for instance, seen in countless movies and appearing, each time as if for the first time, as the announcement of a great promise—is virtually no longer thinkable without the birds-eye view from a plane; and perhaps New York, that quintessential portal to the New World guarded by the Statue of Liberty, is above all the sum total of countless arrivals by boat or by plane, never failing to generate the expectation of being able to start over.

Some people save their dream places for last. Elias Canetti, for example, created a veritable cult around the places he would visit one day. The more sacred a city was to him, the longer he deferred going there. Our ideas about the places we think we might feel comfortable in tend to be both precise and vague at the same time. Like appetite, which makes us salivate, expectation is part memory and part imagination. We always travel in two worlds, the material and the imaginary, and when our body finally arrives at our destination, our mind calls out to it: *Where have you been so long!* That's the magic of foreign places. Don't we all know that wherever we go, others are not the only ones who've already been there. "It's just as I imagined," Goethe famously exclaimed at the sight of Rome, the city of his dreams. Ethnologists have taught us that we tend to project ourselves into all that is foreign and strange and that the dream of remote islands, weathered-faced fishermen, and exotic beaches is mostly inspired by travel guides. But the reverse is equally true: only that which somehow relates to our expectations can be experienced as foreign. Thus, we are a bit like natives who commence their rain dance at the first sight of clouds.

The jetsetter, to whom the planet appears merely as a tangled network of destinations and airport lounges, is today's prototypical traveler. For him, the way from A to B is but an annoying in-between state. Philosopher Günter Anders once described the "business traveler from New York" as the prototypical complainer about the world's anachronisms: "'What a shame', a businessman grumbled as we were flying over Greenland; 'look at all the stuff scattered between Canada and Scotland—it's nothing—expansive, though—just as long as it's *in-between*—and the time! —also nothing—just as long as it's *long*— between departure and arrival, good enough for waiting and napping—what's all this good for anyway!?'"

Mobility is the magic word that translates wanderlust into the bare economics of flexibility, and the traveler who complains about being en route as a necessary evil negates the essential desire tacitly underlying every journey: to come back as a new person. For traveling is still one of the few ways of life where the road is also the goal; and without the troubles of the road the goal would lose its significance. Eros is transitory, it awakens en route, between places, in the force field between departure and arrival. That's why, before every big journey, we still experience some of the excitement we used to feel as children when something unusual was about to happen in our lives.

Traveling means taking time out. And although we may be used to *having been there and done it* already when it comes to most *new* experiences, every major trip into the big wide world still quivers with the agitations of childhood. And whoever doesn't contract the virus of possibility that goes along with traveling forfeits the thrill of the unexpected, which once lay in wait for us around every corner. Even a certain type of obtuseness inherent in waiting belongs to traveling: you have to be able to get lost in order to hit upon the unknown. Most of us, however, have become too complacent not to rely on the travel agent or the web for supplying us with brochures that feature countries and cities as interchangeable as the rooms at the Hilton.

That all roads are, in some way, also detours we feel in places like Venice or Lisbon, where most lanes and alleys end at city walls, bridges, or canals. How could we bear life without travel, which reminds us that sometimes we must get lost to get where, without knowing it, we want to be: this piazza, that façade, or that enchanted panorama we would not have found without making a wrong turn. But roaming is also an end in itself. It follows the distant call of mysterious voices, children playing, the peal of bells of borrowed time. Only one ready to lose himself in the labyrinth enters into the dream that a place dreams of itself, traveling along the songlines that the caravans of generations past have traveled.

Interlude

Developing Baths

My first camera was a square box that you had to hold at chest level in order to see what you were going to shoot through the viewfinder. It made pictures that sometimes captured strange spirits. All this was long ago, though, and I still don't know why this box reproduced reality as a palimpsest. This antiquated device—together with the double-exposed reality it created—was soon superseded by technologically more advanced gadgets. But only digital photography put an end to the uncertainty as to what you would eventually see in the developed picture.What happens if the time it takes to develop a negative in the dark room vanishes? If the unexpected slumbering in the developing bath of our unconscious—like the apparitions in old photographs—no longer comes to light? The surprise at something becoming visible that we hadn't anticipated—a fleeting expression, an involuntary emotion frozen in time, the signs of invisible tension—doesn't stand a chance against the beautiful arrangement. The unpre-

dictable is threatened with extinction, and so is a slice of uncertainty as such. But the more diligently we work toward eliminating chance the faster the host of invisible spirits grows.

Summer in the Country

> Who would deny that the short-cutters and pushers have formed the most efficient psycho-political lobby over the last two thousand years?
>
> (Peter Sloterdijk)

Christianity has assigned waiting a fixed place in the calendar: the four weeks before Christmas are dedicated to Jesus Christ. The promise of his Second Coming opens up a global waiting area that varies slightly from denomination to denomination. This much is agreed upon, though: a better life awaits us after death, and, depending on our behavior, our ordeal in the valley of tears will be compensated for in the hereafter. The first snow sometimes falls around the first Sunday of advent. For a brief period, the world sinks into a deep white sleep; suddenly, all is still, the days are like dreams we are allowed to enter. For most of us, the fact that waiting was once determined by the seasons, that it was tied to the rhythms of agriculture, punctuated only by secular and religious holidays, is merely a distant memory. Greenhouses and globalization have stripped both our produce and the seasons of the specific aromas they once exuded and that tied certain tastes to certain months. Nowadays, you can get Christmas cookies in August. Every advance also implies a loss, and the seasons no longer filter into our memory through our taste buds the way Proust's madeleine once did. Being able to purchase strawberries from May through December comes at a price: they neither smell or taste of anything, nor do they embody memories. To wait for something to ripen has virtually become an anachronism, and typically we have no problem with that. But allowing things to unfold on their own time might also be pleasant for a change—for once, we wouldn't be responsible for the accelerated pace of things.

Still, in certain respects the time signatures of country life remain quite distinct from urban time management, being much more a function of natural conditions (weather, ambient temperature, etc.)—the corn cannot be rushed and hastening the ripening of fruit can only go so far. While our chickens may be forced to lay eggs around the clock, artificial light sources may have reduced the diurnal cycle to a record low, and global warming may soon make winter feel like summer, agriculture, by and large, still follows the seasons. This doesn't mean, however, that the rest and recreation we city dwellers can reasonably expect from a nostalgic *summer in the country* will not be punctuated by the concerted cacophony of all manner of machinery in no way slower than the average speed on the highway—at least not during rush hour.

Interrupting the flow of history, exploding all evolutionary timelines are the hallmarks of modernity. We exist in an on/off mode in which most of the elements constituting the rhythms of nature have been eliminated: repetition and variation, extension and suddenness, in short, the very intervals that give life a melody have been reduced to disturbing interferences. Life in the metropolis has split the continuity of movement into a myriad discontinuities, and the information age has created modes of perception that no longer register becoming. What's strange about all this is that we still feel it. For even though our sensorium may have adapted to the overwhelming speed of today's world, our emotions—that ancient inventory we still rely on as our guide—remain slow, throwing a monkey wrench into the well-oiled machine that is modern life.

Friedrich Nietzsche had already suggested that there might be something wrong with our sensibilities, deploring the atrophied attention span of modern man in the age of the new media. "Now," Nietzsche wrote, "only one kind of seriousness is left in the modern soul: an overwhelming concern with information proliferated by newspapers and the telegraph—it's all about seizing the moment and putting it to use." Echoing Nietzsche,

Walter Benjamin viewed the "rise of the critic, reporter, and photojournalist as emblematic of a cultural development in which *waiting* and *being ready* to point and shoot in the right moment had become the most crucial abilities." When waiting means being on per- manent alert, interaction gives way to information trading and, eventually, raw sensationalism. Thus, the news' "novelty value, brevity [and] lack of internal cohesion," Benjamin concluded, "seal information off against experience."

Perception—the conduit of the past into the present—requires duration, as Henri Bergson pointed out; it needs time. With the advent of the mass media, however, we have adapted to the speed of sensationalism, which has virtually done away with the time necessary to distinguish between what's important and what's not. More often than not, we no longer experience the world itself but, rather, *news* about it. On the news, in turn, systems theorist Niklas Luhmann has argued, "the world only appears as one among other contingencies—as a threefold negation, to be precise: in the sense that the reported events didn't really have to happen, that they didn't really have to be reported, and that we didn't really need to pay attention to them (and, indeed, often enough we don't—when on vacation, for instance)." Since the rise of the Internet, it has probably become somewhat more difficult to turn a blind eye to the news when on vacation. But Benjamin's insight that the selection criteria dictated by the rule of sensationalism "seal information off against experience" still applies.

We live in a world suffering from acceleration compulsion—a world in which, according to sociologist Hartmut Rosa, "people, organizations, and governments find themselves in a state of constant situational reactivity rather than living balanced and creative lives." This rupture in continuity between past, present, and future, which transforms life into a "fatalistic standstill whose quick-paced, changing episodes reveal the eternal recurrence of the same, renders the very notion of creativity meaningless." For living creatively means drawing on and learning from past experience; this, in turn, presupposes conditions for action that are sufficiently stable for us to be able to understand the changes going on around us and actively participate in them. As soon as all options become totalitarian and all possibilities cancel each other out, however, reality dissolves into expectations whose fulfillment always comes both too soon and too late. With the increase in motor power humankind has also increased the heft of its brake pads. Thus, we constantly smuggle pockets of slowness into the fabric of our ever-accelerating lives.

Life Is Too Short

We arrive late and leave early. Mortals that we are, we must both make haste and take it slow—hence, as philosopher Odo Marquard remarks, "all those inevitable congestions on the freeways of our excessive accelerations." If we want to know "how to go about syncing individual slowness with the world's speed," Marquard surmises, "we ought to look to young children, who tend to import the slow rhythms of the familiar into the unfamiliar and fast-paced environments of the world outside by carrying their teddy bears and other *transitional objects* with them wherever they go, thus compensating for their surroundings' foreignness." According to Marquard, adults, too, "especially those with higher education and means, need and have their own *teddy bears* to navigate the challenges of an ever-changing, ever-accelerating modern world"—be they favorite books, music, or devices such as cell phones, iPods, Kindles, and Nooks, which are supposed to make us feel safe by "giving us the sense of always knowing where we're at and what we're dealing with."

This "temporal double life," as Marquard calls it, pervades the individual's daily routine as well as our culture as a whole. And although global acceleration relentlessly works toward eliminating whatever pockets of slowness may remain in our lives—especially those connecting us to the worlds and ways of tradition—paradoxically, we have never spent as much time and money on preserving and appropriating the past as today. Just think of the human hordes bearing down on museums the world over, or of our most recent obsession with memory and memorialization. The "age of landfills is also the age of landmarking," cultural and natural preservation, and sustainability.

Our species is quick and limping, tradition-bound and futuristic, and we simply have to learn to "endure" the tension between our world's growing speed and the "ongoing work of cultural restoration" with a good dose of irony and decorum—so goes the poky hedgehog's lesson to the 'fast and furious' hare. For the faster the new becomes old, the faster the old can become new again, as anyone who has been around the block a couple of times knows. That's why it might actually be "totally okay," Marquard concludes, "calmly to let the others overtake us in history's unremitting marathon and simply wait for history to catch up with us from behind. For we are always both the hedgehog and the hare, and this temporal double life of ours ensures that we neither live exclusively in the fast lane, hungry for the future, nor become the slaves of slow-moving tradition." Otherwise, we wouldn't live our lives to the full, and life is too short for that.

5. LAGGARDNESS

Let It Be

Austrian writer and self-proclaimed "lover of waiting" Peter Handke has emerged as one of the staunchest defenders of slowness in our time. According to Handke, the interplay between waiting for inspiration and doing nothing generates a space in which waiting morphs into "liminal time," which he calls the "hour of true sensation" and which doesn't tell us *what to do* so much as simply to *let it be*. Handke depicts a radiant moment on a bench in Central Park, when, exhausted from a red-eye, he had an epiphany of a world wholly dissolved in waiting: "Late into the night, I did nothing but sit and look; it was as though I didn't even need to breathe." In the "light of his tiredness" the narrator experiences the world's chaos as congealed into the "anodyne of form." This mystical vision—this momentary state of cosmic purposelessness—which implies a calmness of spirit that takes in without evaluating and is in communion with all, is most beautifully captured in a passage from *The Man Without Qualities*, a novel by Handke's fellow Austrian Robert Musil.

"Breathing of a Summer Day" is the title of the posthumous chapter in which the mystical union of the novel's protagonists—the siblings Ulrich and Agathe—is consummated behind the veil of a lusterless flurry of blossoms. "Time stood still, millennia weighed as much as the blink of an eye," as the siblings meditate on a vision of a *temporal double life* constituted by the "appetitive" and the "vegetative." "To the appetitive part," Ulrich explains, "the world owes all works, all beauty, all progress, but also all restlessness, and, finally, also its own meaningless cyclicality;" to the vegetative part it owes "divination and meditation," the twofold source of our greatest happiness. Consequently, there are two modes of action: "We can either burst into tears of rage, happiness, or enthusiasm, like children, and get rid of these emotions in brief, meaningless paroxisms"; or "we can pull ourselves together and not act at our emotions' bidding; in that case, life itself comes to seem like an uncanny dream in which emotion rises past treetops, towers, and all the way to heaven ...!" At this point, the siblings have reached that "magic spirit of idleness" that could also be called contemplation—at the sacred Hour of Pan.

Interlude

Yawning

Why is yawning so contagious? The scent of coffee stimulates our nerves, the scent of fresh pastry our digestion. Another's yawning, on the other hand, compels us to imitate him without affecting us physically in any way. It's as if the tiredness within us had only been waiting for its cue to come out of hiding. As if sleep were waiting in our body ready to pounce, our mouth opens in response to the other's hearty yawn. Even as I'm writing these lines, I am overcome—as if by a repressed urge— by the desire to yawn.

The Hour of Pan

Seeking shelter behind closed lids in the middle of the day has gone out of fashion, except in the hot south, where *siesta* still holds the imaginary promise of erotic adventure. In the midday heat, when time stands still like an impenetrable wall and even the drone of buzzing flies becomes somnolent, drowsiness compels us to lie down. All is silent behind the swelling din of cicadas—as if they were guarding the stillness. Inevitably, we imagine a sparsely furnished room, sunlight filtering through the blind's half-opened slats, a metal-frame bed, rumpled sheets, the sputtering of a moped outside, and a hundred years of solitude ... If there were a compass point for the slow time of somnolence, it would be *south*.

Who really liked taking naps as a child? Even our parents' occasional afternoon naps had something menacing about them, spreading the pall of death over the exuberance of living day. Like paralysis, the injunction to be quiet created an atmosphere of petrified immobility. In *The Dedication*—a novella probing the devastating psychological aftermath of separation—German author Botho Strauß has his protagonist remember his father's afternoon naps, which used to trigger "an anxious rage against God in the boy" just as soon as he'd crack the dining room door and secretly watch his father "asleep upright in his armchair, before he'd come out again with a cup of coffee half an hour later, thus celebrating every afternoon the resurrection of the dead." Could it be that a whiff of this soundless catastrophe hovers over every afternoon nap?

Nowadays, we tend to spend our breaks in gyms and spas, where taking time out and unwinding are geared toward regenerating labor and increasing efficiency. Capitalism has rediscovered the cardinal sin of idleness as a rich source of revenue. Yet only when idleness tips into true leisure does taking time out cease being but a coffee break within the production process (and thus, still governed by it), becoming a genuinely *free* time instead—the net dividend of being alive.

How best to describe such leisure? Perhaps as an instance of memory? For leisure means neither *doing* nor *letting be*; leisure means *being*. Time extended, a vague sense of sinking, sleeping with our eyes open—leisure is certainly closer to happiness than busyness. It allows us to drift into a different temporal dimension where the punch clock doesn't exist. For a brief period, the 'fast and furious' are no longer our business. There's a beautiful old word for it: *laggardness*. Laggardness is a state hailing from an age when time still had fringes, as it were, when it hadn't yet been completely harnessed and functionalized, when it hadn't yet been reduced to a means to an end. Children are laggard; no object, party convention, or train can ever be laggard. And even though 'laggard' may carry negative connotations (implying laziness, or neglect of duty), it does denote those blissful forms of slowness that we typically only indulge in when we are alone.

No clock can measure laggardness, this state of self-oblivion that, just like the word itself, will soon, it seems, be forgotten.

Dwelling on the outskirts of time, it borders on the land of dreams. Building castles in the air, floating downstream in a boat gently rocked by the waves of forgetting, gazing at the clouds—this kind of slowing down enables us to reach beyond waiting, which is not only rife with anxiety and lack but also with the happy anticipation of its own closure, with the possibility of being wholly present without consciousness. That's the promise of sleep.

6. STANDSTILL

Lagoons of Dreams

> Sleep, this seam of your life, which you
> yourself don't possess.
>
> (Jorge Luis Borges)

What is it about the first sentence of Proust's *In Search of Lost Time* that makes it so haunting and memorable? "For a long time I used to go to bed early." These few simple words contain the promise of an incomparable, imaginary world. It's as if the narrator were actively choosing what feels like self-sacrifice in the name of a noble cause. In Proust's oneiric odyssey through time, the narrator is from the outset positioned as the helmsman navigating the lagoons of dreams: the bed is his ship, sleep his sea, and waiting his sail.

Walter Benjamin has pointed out that Proust's "involuntary memory" is much closer to forgetting than to what we typically think of as memory. Proust's "Penelope work of recollection," in which "remembering is the woof and forgetting the warp," is in reality the opposite of the work of Homer's Penelope, its likeness in reverse. For Proust "the day unravels what the night has woven; when we wake up in the morning we hold in our hands but a few … loose strands of the tapestry of lived life, as woven for us by forgetting." Owing to the purposefulness of human agency coupled with the purposive work of waking memory, each day undoes the web, "the ornaments of forgetting." That's why Proust eventually turned his days into nights—so as "not to allow any of those convoluted arabesques to slip through his fingers." The very attempt at fully grasping these beautifully and paradoxically formulated thoughts cannot fail to make one slightly dizzy.

Penelope, meanwhile, hoping day and night for the return of Odysseus, epitomizes a certain mode of waiting coded in female terms and transpiring under the sign of cunning. Pretending to be making a shroud for

Odysseus' old father Laertes, Penelope fends off her suitors by weaving the fabric by day and undoing the day's work by night. She manages to get away with this ruse for three years, until she is betrayed by a servant and her husband returns.

Since "long-suffering Odysseus" set out on the first trip around the world, a woman's waiting had, for the longest time, been tied to ships, as popular songs from as late as the mid-twentieth century attest. Think for instance of Freddy Quinn's 1963 hit record *My Boy, Come Back Again Soon*.* Freddy, whose dark timbre gave voice to a whole generation of 'abandoned', stay-at-home moms, captured the spirit of the times: not the sweetheart on the quay, but the housewife in the kitchen was now in demand. Certainly, this high-seas sailor of the Adenauer era was no brute like Brecht's Surabaya-Johnny—for him, only mother's letters were waiting in

---

* Austrian pop star Freddy Quinn (né Franz Eugen Helmut Manfred Nidl) is remembered in particular for *Junge, komm bald wieder …*

every port: "Wherever the winds may have carried me," he crooned, "I still recall what mother wrote to me. / A letter was waiting in every port / 'Don't be too long' was all she wrote ..." Or think of Nana Mouskouri's 1961 smash hit *The White Rose of Athens* with its memorable chorus: "... till the white rose blooms again, you must leave me, leave me lonely ..." Thus, Freddy was by no means alone on the high seas ... Well into the late 1960s, many a pop song reworked the traditional motif of waiting as the exclusive domain of women, and part of that female core can be said to survive in all waiting.

"Historically speaking," Roland Barthes remarks, "the discourse of absence has always been delivered by women." Women have traditionally given "form to absence, turned it into fiction, for they had the time for it; they wove and sang ... expressing through the hum of the wheel both immobility and absence (the far-away rhythms of distant travels, sea surges, and cavalcades)." Night after night Penelope sends her shuttlecock on its futile journey. The gift of "making beautiful gowns with great intelligence" that she received from Athene—goddess of wisdom and patroness of weaving—is the craft of narrative itself.

Penelope is the classical figure in whom waiting and story-telling are first intertwined, for what she weaves is precisely the story of the wanderings of Odysseus: while his ship is buffeted by storms and disasters—a plaything of fate and divine whim —her shuttlecock, too, drifts back and forth, inscribing the *Odyssey* in her father-in-law's shroud. Penelope's ability to suspend time by 'telling' a story reveals deferral as the very heart and soul of the art of narrative—all the twists and turns in the plot that can virtually outsmart death.

Just in Time

They run into each other after many years at *Shakespeare & Company* in Paris—the last stop on his European book tour. They had first met nine years before on a train to Vienna—he, a young American, she, a French student—and spent a night together before parting at dawn without exchanging anything but the promise to meet again in Vienna six months later. Thus ends Richard Linklater's 1995 romantic comedy *Before Sunrise*.

In the 2004 sequel to *Before Sunrise*, the sun must set before the lovers' longing can be satisfied. *Before Sunset* is a subtle and up-lifting movie, a modern fairy tale about the question: *is there somebody out there, waiting for us?* Two people meet again. They talk, walk, have coffee, take a boat ride on the Seine, and eventually wind up in her apartment. Their conversation is nervous, the veneer of jadedness gradually peels off. Revealed are missed opportunities, the misery of relative contentment. She is skinnier, he has been visibly scarred by life; she has been drifting from relationship to relationship, he is unhappily married with a four-year-old son. When he asks if she's in love with her current boyfriend, she says, "Of course!"

In truth, she has never forgotten the man who first gave her an idea, one early morning in Vienna, of what love is all about. Above all, she loves an idea—the idea of *the one and only*, of two people meant for each other. For, as long as it lasts, love cannot do without the halo of singularity.

They can't believe that they have actually found each other again, here in Paris, after nine years of waiting. At first, they hardly dare to acknowledge their immediately reawakened passion for each other. Their unexpected encounter catapults them back in time, every word they exchange betrays the knowledge that their lives might have been totally different, if only they'd gotten together in Vienna as agreed. Now, however, life lived without the other is both irretrievably past *and* rife with the vague promise of a shared future: here, now, their story begins again. His plane back to New York leaves in eighty minutes. With Nina Simone's *Just in Time* playing in the background, she says, "You're gonna miss that plane." He says, "I know."

Liminal Time

Transition, liminality, growth—puberty, pregnancy, pupation—stages of waiting from which one day a new being will awaken, the stuff of fairy tales. Think of Snow White and Sleeping Beauty, those creatures of waiting—for the latency of desire to morph into embodied sexuality and transience. A young girl falls into a hundred-year-long sleep, and as the years roll by without a trace, something must happen *in time*, something that will trigger her awakening. What valley of oblivion must she traverse in order for Sleeping Beauty to come to as a woman? Into what sleep will our fairy tales' future queens be falling? And with them: the pot roast that stops sizzling, the cook who is about to slap his apprentice—the penalty for a minor offense for decades suspended, the kingdom of a punishment one hundred years in abeyance … This coruscating myth of the 'standstill agreement' with time—oscillating between fear and hope, salvation and punishment—is what all these stories relate. And hadn't we been warned as children—that the grimace will stay as the clock strikes the hour and that we will be forever doomed to wear the grotesque face of disobedience?

Thus, in fairy tales waiting is a curse, and somebody must come—the right one—who is not only capable of scaling the thorny walls of time and the seven hills of jealousy, but who also knows how to outsmart death and lift the glass lid of oblivion for that one critical moment in which the spell is broken and time spits up the poisonous apple. What a genuinely poetic scene: the instant when a person—following a brief, unconscious eternity—looks into the blue eyes of her own future. And don't all the unconscious ones among us—men and women alike— live with the constant risk of suddenly waking up and having to change their lives, if only in literature? As we awaken, however, we again succumb to the law of mortality.

Snow White in her glass coffin has already prefigured the idea of 'cryogenic immortality'—the dream that the freezer will bring reprieve from death. There are people who wish to have their terminally-ill bodies put on ice in order to celebrate their own resurrection on the day when the right kind of treatment for their illness will have been invented. Which calls to mind Johann Peter Hebel's *Unexpected Reunion*—a moving nineteenth-century tale about a young miner and bridegroom in the Swedish city of Falun, who, after a fatal mining accident, is preserved in "ferrous vitriol" for fifty years. This short parable about eternal sleep and unanticipated reunion beyond probability and decay speaks to the collective phantasm of resurrection—the illusion that something could endure and be preserved without falling prey to the implacable tooth of time.

One day, as "the miners at Falun were trying to open up a passage between two shafts, they dug up from the rubble and the vitriol water, a good three hundred yards below ground, the body of a young man soaked in ferrous vitriol but otherwise untouched and unchanged, so that all his features and his age were still recognizable, as if he had died only an hour before or had just nodded off at

work." While he appears as young and intact as he was on the day of the accident, his erstwhile bride-to-be is "grey and bent," having spent her life in the stupor of her fidelity to her beloved. Tethered to the memory of her love, she has witnessed the passage of time, seen wars and generations come and go, until he is unexpectedly returned to her, an old woman, and she can finally lie down with the love of her youth in their "cold wedding bed." It's not at all clear what the moral of the story is supposed to be: that love conquers time and that we'll eventually collect our reward for spending our life waiting, or perhaps the opposite: the devastating insight in view of an exhumed futility that even after a lifetime of waiting the only thing we'll ever get is the beautiful corpse of love's promise.

Time Out

Over the mountain tops
There is peace,
In all the treetops
You feel
Not a breath;
The birds are silent in the wood.
Just wait a little! Soon
You, too, will be at peace.

(Johann Wolfgang Goethe)

Poets know all about the mysteries of sleep:
carried by the wings of desire—"ever homeward bound," as Novalis famously put it
—they know how to hypnotize us with their
rhymes and rhythms, all the while watching
over our awakenings in the "early morning's
downy twilight"—the hour of dawn and betrayal, of lovers and executioners—as another German poet, Eduard Mörike, wrote.

There was a time when night was associated with Romantic desire and Gothic horror. With the rise of modern technology,
however, all this has changed. Domesticated
by electricity, pried open and functionalized

in the light of day, night no longer connotes arousal, fear, and death. Enlightenment's illuminations now burn as electrical installations. "From dream research to global transportation," Peter Sloterdijk notes, "the modern world is ruled by the law of night work." One could even go so far as to say that "when we go to sleep at night it's not we who take a break from the world, but, rather, it's the world that takes a break from us." What hasn't changed, though, is that from the day we are born we still can't help existing according to the oscillating "rhythms of waking and sleeping, presence and absence," being there and being gone.

The cradle rocks above an abyss—and that's precisely what we, enlightened creatures of "night-deprived thinking," seem to be rather unwilling to admit. "If we could finally strike the word 'God'," Sloterdijk muses, "only the world's specific 'time out' would be left, its break, its discreet nothing"—eliminating God, however, is impossible, for even in his absence he would remain powerfully present.

In this life, meanwhile, there is no more perfect mode of presence-in-absence than sleep —the preserve of our former lives. Feelings of extreme happiness, or overwhelming hatred, emotions as pure as only childhood knows them, are all preserved in our sleep, in whose crepuscular expanses the dead wait for us as well. At night, we communicate with our ghosts; and if they happen to mingle with the living in our dreams (resembling one, acting like another, including ourselves) as in old, double-exposed photographs, in the morning we will most likely be haunted for hours on end by the vague feeling that the practical distinction we make between dreaming and reality might be misguided, if no doubt reassuring. Sleep is our subtenant for life. In it, waiting, which is what our life is, has found its most enduring expression. But maybe we got it all backwards: maybe we are the dream that the dead dream?

Martin Heidegger spoke of the "forbearance of Being" in an attempt to capture the specific kind of slowing down that allows us to probe the meaning of our very being. All

important, existential questions about what it means to be wedged between natality and mortality, between the brief span of our *lifetime* and the millennia of *world time*—suspended in waiting—are invariably tied to this kind of "forbearance." We are "beings begun," but the meaning of life only becomes transparent to us in light of its end point, toward which we are constantly oriented. Yet, we can only exist by pretending that it can be indefinitely deferred; and although, under an empty heaven, most of us probably no longer expect to find a better world in the afterlife, we can't seem to be able to do without substitutes just yet.

Siegfried Kracauer detected a "profound sadness" in his Weimar contemporaries and read it as a direct corollary of humanity's "exile from the religious sphere." In his seminal 1922 essay *The Ones Waiting*, he chastised all the new ideologies peddled by cultural prophets, activists, and social reformers by way of surrogate secular religions—from Nietzsche's superman doctrine, to Ernst Bloch's messianic communism, to Max Weber's theory of cultural disenchantment. Kracauer cautiously pleaded for an "attitude of waiting" instead. Whoever adopts this attitude, he suggested, "neither forecloses the possibilities of faith like the staunch nihilist, nor does he put all his eggs in one basket like the desperate believer. He waits, and his waiting is a 'cautious openness,' in a sense difficult to explain." If his "attitude of waiting" didn't still betray the vestiges of a profound longing for and belief in the possibility of salvation, Kracauer might be called a cautiously judicious pragmatist. But—there is no way back, and, all religious revivals notwithstanding, no new dawn is looming on the theological horizon. With all our bloody attempts at implementing utopias on earth having failed and the lifelines of faith virtually capped, we seem to have nothing left but the hollow shell of existence. The best we can do is hope that one day, provided we are patient, we'll find ourselves living in a better and more hospitable world—it being understood that this seemingly naïve belief in a 'brighter' future is itself already part of the very future it would bring about. So long as we keep such fictions alive we know that we aren't yet paralyzed by the factual—and who knows, perhaps they will have contributed to the occasional realization of some of our dreams at least.

Let there be light, God said, and there was light, without delay. Unconditional fulfillment, immediate gratification are core components of the very notion of paradise, and every time our desires happen to be promptly satisfied, we step back into paradise with one foot. However, given that we have unlimited desires in a limited lifetime, we can never satisfy them all. The delay between wish and wish fulfillment is an essential part of our condition. With our appearance in this world, the umbilical cord, through which milk and honey once flowed unbidden, has been irreversibly cut. And every time our wishes are granted too easily or quickly, a vengeful God exacts his due: we forfeit the rewards of patience. Caerus, the lucky moment, presupposes waiting—the gift of time passing time

—excruciatingly long sometimes, and sometimes blissfully wasted, but always a gift.

BIBLIOGRAPHY

- Günther Anders, *Die Antiquiertheit des Menschen [The Obsoleteness of Man]* (1980).
- Roland Barthes, *Fragments d'un discours amoureux [Fragments of a Lover's Discourse]* (1977).
- Charles Baudelaire, *Les Fleurs du mal [The Flowers of Evil]* (1857).
- Samuel Beckett, *Waiting for Godot* (1953).
- Walter Benjamin, *Illuminationen [Illuminations]* (1977).
- Henri Bergson, *Matière et mémoire [Matter and Memory]* (1896).
- Maurice Blanchot, *L'attente l'oubli [Expectation Oblivion]* (1962).
- Hans Blumenberg, *Lebenszeit und Weltzeit [Life Time and World Time]* (1986).
- Albert Camus, *Le Mythe de Sisyphe [The Myth of Sisyphus]* (1942).
- Paul Celan/Ilana Schmueli, *Briefwechsel [Correspondence]* (2004).
- Emil Cioran, *Précis de décomposition [A Brief History of Decay]* (1949).
- Gustave Flaubert, *Madame Bovary* (1857).
- Michel Foucault, *Surveiller et punir: naissance de la prison [Discipline and Punish: The Birth of the Prison]* (1975).

- Sigmund Freud, *Jenseits des Lustprinzips [Beyond the Pleasure Principle]* (1921).
- Wilhelm Genazino, *Der gedehnte Blick [The Extended Gaze]* (2004).
- Peter Handke, *Versuch über die Müdigkeit [Essay on Tiredness]* (1989).
- Johann Peter Hebel, *The Treasure Chest: Stories*, translated by John Hibberd (1995).
- Martin Heidegger, *Grundbegriffe der Metaphysik [Basic Concepts of Metaphysics]* (1929/2004).
- Heinrich Heine, *Vermischte Schriften [Selected Writings]* (1997).
- Franz Kafka, *Der Prozeß [The Trial]* (1925).
- Siegfried Kracauer, *Ausgewählte Schriften [Selected Writings]*(1990).
- Niklas Luhmann, *Soziologische Aufklärung [Sociological Enlightenment]* (1972).
- Odo Marquard, *Skepsis und Zustimmung [Skepticism and Agreement]* (1994).
- Friedrich Nietzsche, *Die fröhliche Wissenschaft [The Happy Science]* (1882).
- -----, *Jenseits von Gut und Böse:Vorspiel einer Philosophie der Zukunft [Beyond Good and Evil: Prelude to a Philosophy of the Future]* (1886).
- -----, *Unzeitgemäße Betrachtungen [Untimely Meditations]* (1876).
- Hartmut Rosa, *Beschleunigung: Die Veränderung der Zeitstrukturen in der Moderne [Acceleration: The Transformation of the Structures of Time in the Modern Age]* (2005).

- Manfred Schneider, *Love and Betrayal [Liebe und Betrug]* (1992).
- Botho Strauß, *Die Widmung [The Dedication]* (1977).
- Peter Sloterdijk, *Weltfremdheit [Unworldliness]* (1993).
- -----, *Zorn und Zeit [Rage and Time]* (2006).
- Stendhal [Marie Henri Beyle], *De l'amour [On Love]* (1822).
- Harald Weinrich, *Knappe Zeit: Kunst und Ökonomie des befristeten Lebens [Limited Time: The Art and Economy of Life Limited]* (2004).
- Dieter Wellershoff, *Die Arbeit des Lebens [The Work of Life]* (1985).
- D. W. Winnicott, *Playing and Reality* (1971).

ABOUT THE AUTHORS

ANDREA KÖHLER is a cultural correspondent for the Swiss daily newspaper *Neue Züricher Zeitung* and the recipient of the 2003 Berlin Book Critics Prize. She lives in New York City

A frequent contributor to *The New York Review of Books*, MARK LILLA teaches at Columbia University and is the author of, among other books, *The Stillborn God: Religion, Politics, and the Modern West* and *The Shipwrecked Mind: On Political Reaction*.

MICHAEL ESKIN is an award-winning translator and author of, among other books, *Poetic Affairs: Celan, Grünbein, Brodsky* and *The Wisdom of Parenthood: An Essay*.

AVAILABLE & FORTHCOMING FROM UWSP

- *The Wisdom of Parenthood: An Essay*
  by Michael Eskin
- *A Moment More Sublime: A Novel* by Stephen Grant
  (2015 Independent Publisher Book Award for
  Contemporary Fiction)
- *High on Low: Harnessing the Power of Unhappiness*
  by Wilhelm Schmid (2015 Living Now Book
  Award for Personal Growth & 2015
  Independent Publisher Book Award for Self-
  Help)
- *Become a Message: Poems* by Lajos Walder
  (2016 Benjamin Franklin Book Award for
  Poetry)
- *What We Gain As We Grow Older: On Gelassenheit*
  by Wilhelm Schmid
- *On Dialogic Speech* by L. P. Yakubinsky
- *Passing Time: An Essay on Waiting*
  by Andrea Köhler
- *In Praise of Weakness* by Alexandre Jollien
- *Vase of Pompeii: A Play* by Lajos Walder
- *Below Zero: A Play* by Lajos Walder
- *Tyrtaeus: A Tragedy* by Lajos Walder
- *The Complete Plays* by Lajos Walder
- *Homo Conscius: A Novel* by Timothy Balding
- *Castile: A Novel* by Stephen Grant
- *Potentially Harmless: A Philosopher's Manhattan*
  by Kathrin Stengel

Designed by UWSP
Printed in the United States of America